Aug 2013

"BUT I DON'T SEE YOU AS ASIAN"

CURATING CONVERSATIONS ABOUT RACE

Chips,

Thanks for the support and I hope this helps in Greater Atlanta bridge.

Peace,

Bruce Reilly

Early praise - "But I don't see you as Asian"

Bruce pushes back without pushing over.
Chuck Goodman, Pastor, Springfield, IL

◆

Reyes-Chow goes where few people can on the matter of race. He points out land mines, expresses the tension of living in the midst of them, and yet is able to teach us all how to dance, to move more freely with one another. He writes as a humble teacher, neither Black or White, but human and in color.
David Park, nextgenerasianchurch.com

◆

... a no nonsense, no-need-to-decipher work on race and ethnicity with a message of ... rendered up in digestible portions allowing for a 21st century nuanced read on race.
Kimberly Erwin, MS Intercultural Communication, University of Pennsylvania

◆

Using both personal anecdotes and astute cultural references...an entry point into needed conversations while exposing the fears and anxieties that often make these dialogues difficult and awkward. At times silly, other times insightful, this resource is the primer for thoughtful engagement on a subject many prefer to ignore.
Derrick Weston, Director, Coretta Scott King Center, Antioch College, OH

◆

We have spent far too long ignoring our privilege and acting as if racism will work itself out. Bruce's approach allows individuals and communities to tackle deep prejudice and ignorance in a way that will make change in our families, neighborhoods, and churches."
Rev. Abby King-Kaiser, Assistant Director for Ecumenical and Multi-faith Ministry, Dorothy Day Center for Faith and Justice at Xavier University, OH

As a white, Appalachian male, Bruce angers me, challenges me, informs me, comforts me. This is a must read for those of us -- white, brown, black, whatever -- who strive every day to bring a truly equitable society to reality.

John Bolt, Presbyterian Ruling Elder and Director of University Relations/News, West Virginia University

◆

...a succinct, graceful challenge to specific games we play to distance ourselves from doing our own work... unveiling another wire in the birdcage of racism usually invisible to the dominant culture.

Tim Nafziger, Assistant Director, Christian Peacemaker Teams

◆

... continuing the conversation and providing a space to ask, does race matter? And confirming for me... yes it does, and here is why.

Camille Turner-Townsend, Radio Host, iconoklastradio.com and Doctorate Student, New York Theological Seminary

◆

... engages readers in a conversational tone to not just think about race but also to talk about it. I would recommend anyone remotely or actively thinking about race to read this book...

Rachel Helgeson, Lilly Pastoral Resident, First Presbyterian Church, Dallas

◆

In contrast to responding to racial difference with color-blindness, Bruce suggests there is a response that is more authentic and has greater integrity, to recognize racial differences as expressions of the diversity and giftedness...

Christina Auch, Seminary Student

◆

... a tour de force answer to the face of the most common myths and misconceptions regarding race relations in the U.S.

Jarret Chin, Platform Assistant, Unity Church, CA

...a much needed entry point for individuals and groups beginning to think about intersectionality...a balance of theory and experience, critical analysis and grace. For those of us willing to have a conversation about race and racism, Bruce comes alongside and offers his vantage point as a lens without trying to speak for others.

Katie Mulligan, A Ministry of Many

◆

...a thoughtful conversation partner whether your community is just beginning an exploration about race, or is in need of new ways for fruitful paths forward for church and society.
But I Don't See You as Asian delivers.

Rev. Linda Stewart-Kalen, pastor and participant in Portland's Presbyterian Urban Network.

◆

Bruce compels all of us who fancy ourselves activists and rabble rousers to think carefully and engage courageously our intentions, interactions, and personal and institutional behaviors regarding questions of diversity and race.

Elizabeth Shannon, Associate Director of the Center for Spiritual Life and Associate Chaplain, Eckerd College, FL and Co-Moderator, Presbyterian Peace Fellowship

◆

For see complete reviews and/or to offer your own:

http://goo.gl/rG46X

"But I Don't See You as Asian"
Curating Conversations about Race

By Bruce Reyes-Chow

Dedication

This book is dedicated to my grandparents, Chuck, May, Marie, and Esteban, without whose courage, perseverance, feistiness, devotion, humor, and love I would not be who or where I am today.

Pinned

All illustrations and statistics referenced, as well as other helpful resources, can be found on this Pinterest board. This list will be updated periodically, so if any resources should be added, please let me know via any of the links in the "Stay in Touch" section at the end of the book.

http://goo.gl/8cQL4

Table of Contents

Acknowledgments

The writing of this book would not have been possible without the patience and support of my family: my wife, Robin, and my daughters, Evelyn, Abby, and Annie; the support of our church, school, and extended family; and the gifts of the book team: Ryan, Lauren, and Laura.

And for supplying me with my daily caffeine and food intake, big props to the baristas at Philz Coffee and Java on Ocean in San Francisco and I.V. Coffee Lab in Incline Village, Nevada.

Thank you all.

Lorenzo

A few years after I graduated from high school, I received news that one of my classmates, Lorenzo White, had been killed.

Lorenzo was one of the very first people that I met when I started attending Luther Burbank High School, which was outside of my district but had started a new program to help diversify the school. In other words, this school consisted primarily of students of color and poor students, and they wanted to bring in middle-class kids from other parts of Sacramento. While I was not happy about going there, in hindsight I see that going to that school changed my life.

As I remember it, Lorenzo was one of those guys that could easily be described as a man-child. Big, playful, and I'm pretty sure could grow facial hair before I learned to walk. Lorenzo was smart and African-American, and he was one of the first people to extend his hand to me in friendship.

My greatest memories of Lorenzo revolve around us causing trouble in chemistry class. For what it's worth, I firmly believe that giving smart and smart-assed teenage boys Bunsen burners is not a good idea. Along with our other creative classmates, we used to do things like heat up keys or quarters and put them on the floor to see if anyone would pick them up.

Yeah, hilarious.

When you consider all of the things that we did, many of which could be labeled "stupid," I am surprised that we did not singe our eyebrows, melt off our fingerprints, or cause any school-wide evacuations.

We did come close, however.

One afternoon during class, we thought it would be cool to see what happened if we stuffed a rubber stopper down the neck of a flask of something in the midst of a chemical reaction. We were sure it would act like a cannon, shooting the rubber stopper across the room, fueled by the pressure built up by the reaction.

That's *not* what happens.

Turns out a rubber-stoppered flask will explode before it projects the stopper across a classroom. As we stood there with humbled faces and blue liquid all over our white Miami Vice jackets, someone gave Lorenzo his new nickname: the Black Smurf.

Good times with a good person.

While he hung out with many of us during school, we didn't do much together outside of school. I do remember, however, that he was never part of the conversations about college, the future, or other "dreams" that should be part of every young person's life at that age. Lorenzo came from a community and a family situation that were different than mine. My family was middle-class Asian-American; his was working-class African-American. My community always pointed toward and built an expectation that I would be going to college, and his future was one that seemed to have little support or direction. Of course, at fourteen, fifteen, sixteen, I was pretty oblivious to the realities that existed for other people and not for me.

Upon hearing of Lorenzo's death, my high school friends and I were saddened, shocked, but shamefully unsurprised that Lorenzo's life had ended this way. Lorenzo's was one of those stories that you hear about all the time: smart kid gets caught up in bad stuff and ends up dead. We hear stories like this so often, and then, obedient, content consumers, we allow ourselves to be led to the next story by a fickle and short-attention-spanned news cycle.

> *Doing good in the world is a challenge and a choice that is laid before us each and every day. We simply need to decide if we will choose to accept it.*

Whenever I think about doing good in the world, when it would be easier to remain silent or unaware, not only are my own children are always pushing and prodding me forward, I also force myself to look back and remember Lorenzo.

For some reason, even after twenty-five-plus years have passed, Lorenzo's death has stayed with me. After he died, a group of classmates with whom I stayed in touch and I asked ourselves the usual questions: "What could have been done?" "Why did it happen?" and "What do we do now?"

While I know that the risk of compassion fatigue is always high in our überconnected world, it is not an option for me to simply give in to the idea that this is the way things will always be or that there's nothing I can do. There are Lorenzos all around us: people, situations, strangers, and friends requiring us to stay engaged and keep trying to make the world a better place.

This calling is not about being saviors of those whom we decide need to be saved; it is about doing that which helps bring life, joy, and hope to others and, as a result, bettering all of our lives. It is not about serving others so we can pat ourselves on the back; it's about understanding our own privilege and access in ways that help right injustice in the world. Doing good in the world is a challenge and a choice that is laid before us each and every day. We simply need to decide if we will choose to accept it.

Of course, this posture of living to do good can seem idealistic and naïve, but the alternative is to decide that you and I have been placed on this earth only for our own good and have no responsibility toward or connection with those around us. Not only do I think that this is short-sighted, but also that it sells each of us short, for I choose to believe that every person has the potential to be a powerful person of change and transformation in the world.

As I will share, because of the ways the world understands and interacts about race, this is one issue that we cannot give up on, get tired of, or believe we are past. Whether or not there was anything my friends and I could have done about Lorenzo, I have no doubt that being Black in the United States played a significant role in the ultimate results of his life, just as it does in the lives of many people of color today.

> *This offering, in memory of my friend Lorenzo, is my contribution to our communal journey.*

I will be the first to admit that embracing racial diversity in the United States can create both joy and frustration, but if we don't commit to continue to talk about issues of race, then we will only perpetuate explicit and institutionalized racism and cultural exclusion. And when we let this happen, not only will the Lorenzos of the world be unable to reach their fullest potential, but also each and every one of us will lose out on the beauty that healthy, genuine racial diversity can bring to the world.

For this reason, as has been the case for generations, we as a country, culture and a society — whether we are discussing class, gender, sexuality, religion, physical ability, or, in this case, race — must keep talking, keep reflecting, and keep engaged on the winding path that is community.

This offering, in memory of my friend Lorenzo, is my contribution to our communal journey.

Introduction

It is the 1940s, just after the end of World War II, and a young, brown-skinned woman steps onto a bus in Little Rock, Arkansas. As she turns to take a seat, she is faced with a dilemma: *Where should I sit?*

There she stands, a Brown woman trying to navigate the Black-and-White-segregated South. The bus driver, apparently thinking she is White, motions for her to sit in the front of the bus. The woman, knowing she is not White, feels a deeper connection to the Black folks on the bus and feels drawn to those sitting in the back.

The woman was Maria Averas, my grandmother, and she had just arrived from the Philippines. She was brought to the United States as a war bride and then eventually abandoned in Arkansas.

She sat in the back.

Fast-forward to the 1970s. A young boy in Sacramento, California, is given an art assignment: "Draw a self-portrait." Maybe he hears the instructions incorrectly or maybe he thinks he is being clever, but what this crayon-wielding seven-year-old produces is a coolie-hat-wearing, buck-toothed, slanty-eyed character named Pup E. Chow with the tagline, "I like dogs."

Yes, this boy was me and I drew this picture in the 1970s, when stereotypes about Asian immigrants eating dogs were at their height.

That's right, my self-portrait, Pup E. Chow, wears a coolie hat, has slanty eyes and buck teeth, and likes dogs. (A picture is on the final page of the book)

Zip forward just a few more decades. A young mother is pushing her toddler around a church conference in the beautiful mountains of North Carolina. An older White lady in her sixties stops to admire the young mother and her child, cooing, "Your baby is beautiful. Where is she from?"

The mother thinks, "Oh, how sweet — she sees my

daughter as an individual, a person with her own story, her own journey, her own life." So she answers, "San Francisco."

Clearly this is not the response that the lady is seeking, for, with a puzzled look and a hint of condescension, she asks one more time, hoping to get at what she really want to know. "No, where is she FROM?"

And then it hits the young mother, a White woman herself, as well as the woman who birthed this child who is currently observing the summer sky from the safety of her stroller. She gets it. This question is not meant to be an empowering inquiry into her child's identity; it is about the color of her skin.

The child in that stroller was our oldest daughter, Evelyn. Evelyn, who is a little Chinese, a little Filipino, a dash of Spanish, and 50 percent tenth-generation White American, was born in San Francisco, in California, in the United States of America.

"No, where is she FROM?"

This question was posed innocently enough and certainly not with malice. What she wanted to know—I presume what my daughter's ethnic background was—is not a bad thing to be curious about. But ultimately, this question is a stark reminder that skin color still determines how people initially perceive place, belonging, and identity in the United States.

It should be no surprise that this was not an isolated incident. After hearing "Where is she from?" over and over again, my wife has perfected her response.

"No, where is she FROM?

"From my womb."

Cue awkward and appropriate silence.

> ...I am a firm believer in living out what my wise mother often told us: "Make good choices," and "Don't be a knucklehead."

And then there are the random people who have come up to my wife or me and shared adoption stories: "Your daughter is so cute. A couple from our church adopted a baby girl from China." Adoption stories are wonderful stories, but this is not the story of our children.

And then there was the time we saw a person walking down the street, dressed up for Halloween. His costume: a buck-toothed, slanty-eyed coolie.

Pup E. Chow lives!

And then there was time that a truck pulled up beside my family's car at a stop sign. The driver, with his fingers pulling back the corners of his eyes, yelled, "Chink!" followed by a couple seconds of some "ching-chong" gibberish meant to mock Asian languages.

And then there was the time a family member told me that he liked my African-American friend because he was not like other Blacks.

And then there was the time when a classmate told my daughter that she was not Filipino enough.

And then there was the time that I went to my favorite café to find the ever-so-creative and charming "Fuck that chink!" graffitied on the side of the building

> *...we must not be naïve when we approach conversations about race. These topics can be dangerous.*

And then there are the times people comment on my blogs, saying, "Go back to your country."

Or the times when I meet someone who apparently has nothing else to say, who questions or comments on my Asianness.

And then... and then... and then...

My stories are not unique. In fact, for many non-White people growing up in the United States, I would hazard a guess that my stories are fairly generic. Things happen, we try to respond well, and we move on... until the next time.

And thus, even before my birth, navigating events driven by race, ethnicity, and skin color were part of my life. I have tried not to let these occurrences make me feel jaded about humanity or drive me into a bubble of cynicism and outrage. Instead I have tried to employ a posture of righteous indignation when appropriate and compassion and understanding when necessary, always maintaining a foundational belief that there is goodness at the core of each and every person.

We may not always operate out of that goodness, but I choose to believe that the best version of every individual is always fighting to be expressed and set free—for to believe otherwise, that people inherently lack the capacity for good, excuses avoiding dealing with the world and is a posture of living that I refuse to pass on to my children.

But wait. Lest anyone label and dismiss me as some idealistic Pollyanna, some San Francisco hippie: I am no Pollyanna. Following the ways of the world, interactions are too often filled with malice and mean-spiritedness, and I am a firm believer in living out what my wise mother often told us: "Make good choices," and "Don't be a knucklehead."

I love that lady.

While I believe everyone has the capacity to do good and should generally be given the benefit of the doubt, I also believe we also must be wise when we approach interactions and situations that could potentially present physical or emotional harm.

While I would like to believe that we, a society have outgrown instigating and accepting behaviors that incite and encourage violence based on race, culture, or religion, we need only consider the 2013 Boston Marathon bombings to see that this is not the case. While there were great examples of compassion, courage, and love shown that day, and while some news agencies, individuals, and organizations started out with great restraint, much of the commentary quickly devolved into making Muslims scapegoats, attacking people of Middle Eastern descent — perceived or actual — and creating an atmosphere hostile to anyone who dared to challenge the hostility being created in the name of nationalism.

Terms like "towel head," "camel jockey," and "sand nigger," tossed around by people young and old, white and brown, showed that we, as a country, are still a long way from being anywhere near postracial, despite great strides in some areas. So often coupled with threats of violence and retribution, these terms made it abundantly clear that we must not be naïve when we approach conversations about race. These topics can be dangerous. Even those who are experienced with these discussions know that talking about race is

> *Our fear of broaching the topic of race and the difficult conversations that may follow must no longer keep us from having the conversation in the first place.*

difficult, produces strong feelings, and must be approached with a tender heart, a disciplined mind, and a flexible spirit.

So while it might be an attractive option to avoid the topic altogether, we must not buy into the cultural norm that seems to be overtaking communities of thoughtful people: "Don't talk about hard things." As is the case with politics, religion, and sporting allegiances, it may be professionally prudent and socially acceptable to avoid talking about race, but nobody promised that being in a community would be easy or without struggle. If families, communities, and governments hope to experience healing and wholeness, avoiding the emotional, difficult, or painful is not a sustainable or life-giving strategy.

We must commit, as communities and as a country, to talking about race.

We as a society are like a couple struggling in their relationship. We have reached the end of our rope and have given up on the — pick your metaphor — "melting pot," "fruit salad," "tapestry," or "mosaic" experiment that has been the ongoing narrative of our country. We cannot afford *not* to talk about race. Otherwise, we are like the struggling couple who says that they don't have the time, money, or energy to go to counseling.

One of the reasons that I am writing this book is because I truly believe, contrary to what the pundits and politicians would have us believe, that when thoughtful people gather together, we have the capacity to hold passionate, personal, transformative conversations, even about race.

That said, I think one reason that having these conversations is so difficult is because we have forgotten how to even try. When we have attempted to talk about race in the past, it has not gone well.

Our fear of broaching the topic of race and the difficult conversations that may follow must no longer keep us from having the conversation in the first place. If we, as an increasingly diverse people, are going to move forward with a deeper appreciation for the complexities that race brings to society, we must risk having conversations about race. For when we are faced with anxiety, a posture of "What might be possible if we try?" is more likely to lead us to discovering new forms of community than starting with "This won't matter, so let's not even bother," condemning the endeavor to failure.

So the foundational question before us is, "Why talk about race?"

Again, talking about race is difficult. Tackling the topic often draws out the worst of our society and can incite those who thrive in a culture of dehumanization and bullying. I also see the attraction to hunkering down, finding a safe and comfortable theo-ideo-sociological bubble and never leaving. Ever. You need only read comments on any blog about race to see the ugliness and hatred that people demonstrate toward one another.

So again, "Why?" is a valid question. I have blogged about race over the years and received some rather colorful comments. If I were to include them here, I would have to slap an explicit-content label on the cover, so trust me when I say that the hate and ugly that many fear encountering are very real.

> ...when we choose to dismiss or avoid these difficult conversations, we reinforce and remind people of color that they are still the "other."

These are some of the things people have said to me when I tried to engage others, haters included, in conversations about race:

"Just ignore them."

"Don't give them power."

"That is just one person; not all people feel this way. Let it go."

"Stop being so sensitive."

"Everyone is excluded by someone."

"You're not special, so get over it."

"Don't complain. You have it pretty good."

"You should be grateful for what you have — at least it's not like it used to be."

"If you would *stop* talking about race, maybe we would get over racism."

"Don't be so angry."

"Don't say anything."

"Oh, you should have said something."

I have heard all these sentiments before, usually from well-meaning people I know yearn to discover a genuine place of racial harmony and reconciliation. But to be honest, most of the conversations about race that I have had in predominantly White contexts end up supporting and justifying the fact that, in the United States, White is still considered the norm. I choose to believe that this outcome is generally unintended and subconscious, but when we choose to dismiss or avoid these difficult conversations, we reinforce and remind people of color that they are still the "other." We are not expressing a willingness and yearning to embrace the wonderful complexity that is brought to the larger human family, but just the opposite — we are saying, "After all you have done, after all these years, after everything that we've done for you... when we look at you, we still see the 'other.'"

Passive otherness is further encouraged with messages like, "Be grateful for what you DO have," "Don't rock the boat," and "Race doesn't matter." These statements avoid difficult realities; they further divide a people claiming and striving to be one.

No matter how we look at it, being the other in the United States is not good.

"But *everyone* experiences racial otherness, even us White folks," is a common response to this idea. And I agree, to a point. Regardless of our social and cultural contexts, we all face times when we are the others in the room. I hear stories coming from urban settings or college campuses where White folks feel excluded because of the color of their skin. I will tackle this issue later, but I still argue that people of color in the United States today continue to face a particular kind of otherness that White folks will never be able to fully experience or understand. And whether you agree with me on this or not, through the statements that I attempt to unpack, I hope my reasons for holding these beliefs will be made clearer.

To expand a little more, the kind of "otherness" I am describing shows up in church, school, media, and politics, among other places, and it is not something to be ignored. Just like that couple who can't make the time to see a counselor, if we do not tackle our problems head-on, we will condemn ourselves to the building up of resentment, anger and distrust. These will continue to subtly play out in social and political institutions as well as express themselves in widespread physical violence. Yes, we have come a long way, but in many ways, the racial issues and racist results remain the same.

Finally, we must keep talking about race and how we engage the conversation, because how we do these things impacts the ability for people of color to fully live and achieve in society. I am reminded of this reality every morning as my babies wake up to face and embrace the day. Conversations on race matter because we are raising three girls in a very male-centered, hypersexualized world that exoticizes and makes assumptions about them because of their race. It also matters because the legacy we help create about important things like race, class, sexuality, faith, politics, and the environment will impact our children and future generations.

So the answer to the question "Why?" is this: if we do not talk, things will not change.

Now, for those who make a living and gain influence from sustained division — I am looking at you, TV pundits Bill O'Reilly and Jon Stewart — sustaining and feeding these cultural tensions are just fine and even encouraged. But most of us, who are simply trying to live and thrive in a culture of understanding and complexity, must seek out and embody a better way.

Yes, we may be weary of the arguing that has already taken place, fearful of the conflicts that might arise, or doubtful that anything will come of our attempts, but I implore you not to give up trying to talk about it. While the cost in relationships, energy, and status could potentially be significant, the potential for lives to be saved, healing to be had, and hope to be restored is worth any risk you take.

So if you are up for it, I invite you enter the important conversation about race.

Chapter 1

Words to Begin

Before I get into the crux of the book, I want to acknowledge that starting this dialogue means leading people down a path fraught with personal dangers and communal landmines, fueled by the reality that race is incredibly complex, inherently subjective, and deeply personal.

One of the most difficult aspects of a conversation about race is acknowledging that our particular social and cultural contexts influence our overall experiences of race and the conversations that follow. When we are talking about such a personal, complex topic, our contexts and perspectives are just as important as working through the specific questions themselves.

For this reason, I want to lay out and claim as many of my own contextual realities as I can, as honestly and as completely as I can. As I will share later, the things that make me uniquely me will undoubtedly create unintended biases and assumptions. I don't always know what they all are or how they will impact my worldview and conclusions, but I do know I have them and embrace the fact that they are woven throughout this book.

I don't undertake this exercise of transparency to deny the lenses through which I see and write or to defend anything that I might say. I do so in order to claim these things as vital and viable parts of the conversation as a whole, and hope that you, the reader, will endeavor to do the same.

Intent

Like any author, I went back and forth, noodling over the title of this book. There was an ongoing battle in my head between, *No, where are you FROM?* and *Words*

Matter, but I eventually landed on *But I don't see you as Asian.* Oh, but that pesky subtitle.

I went through several iterations before I finally docked for good at the simple, *Curating Conversations about Race.* I have no delusions about my power or ability to teach the world how solve all conflicts born out of race relations, and I do not believe that I have stumbled upon a "ten easy steps to racial reconciliation" plan that will transform society into a multicultural utopia where we will dine on the fruits and drink of racial harmony and cultural bliss. Instead, I hope to set the table so we can sit together as a human family, to provide some context for meaningful discussion, and to curate a space conducive for all people to regularly inquire, engage, and be transformed.

> *My hope is that this book will provide a foundation upon which we may build better day-to-day conversations about race, which may in turn lead to more in-depth intellectual study or outward social action.*

This book is intended neither as a deeply intellectual academic classroom, nor as a passionate and provocative protest march. While I value both of those mediums and their importance to larger race conversations, I am hoping to find that sweet middle space where, after our intellect is stirred in the classroom and our hearts moved on the picket line, we can sit down to eat, drink, and commune. Yes, we can still be passionate about what we believe, but the commitment to be a community who can sit together and break bread around a table is our driving force and motivation — to say it another way, I hope that we can, together, become a healthy space for conversations about race.

When setting up the structure and driving content of the book, I chose statements and comments that people have made to me or that I have heard people say to others. Most of the speakers did not make these comments with impunity or malice; these words are simply representative of what folks often say. These same folks then become confused and dismayed when their words cause someone to take a pause at best or deeply offend someone at worst.

I did not include any of the many statements that have been "shared" with me with the sole intention to outrage, incite, and dehumanize. We can easily dismiss these kinds of comments, because those who choose to make them have little genuine interest in finding common ground or building community. No, the statements that made the final cut were those that, regardless of intent, created resentment, hostility, and division within a community that genuinely seeks understanding, compassion, and wholeness.

By lifting up these statements, unpacking them a bit, and then reframing the conversations about them, I hope to help people engage the tensions that might arise in order to get to the other side of the conflict and achieve understanding — so that, you know, we don't just talk about stuff, but instead start to grow in the course of new, helpful conversations about race.

In choosing the word "curating," I don't intend to claim the status of guru, make grandiose assumptions about my cultural influence, or punch my ticket on the "cool word of the moment" train. Instead, I hope my words embody the best of what it means to assemble a collection in a museum and do so in a way that inspires inquiry and instigates conversation. Just as a museum curator gathers together a collection of items meant to bring an increased depth of understanding to a particular topic, for each statement that I lift up, I hope to bring together big-picture concepts, personal examples, and nuanced interpretations to help us get closer to understanding the issue of race and its impact on personal relationships.

The curator prepares the room with essential items, but also continues to care for that room once it is set up. At the end of the day and at the end of this book, I hope to have equipped readers with illustrations and general insights that they can transfer and translate into personal interactions and relationships that are nuanced, particular, and expansive.

I also hope along the way, as I share my stories about race, folks can find points of connection that might compel and encourage them to tell their own stories—for if we are to have healthy and helpful conversations about race, we must each risk adding our own voice to the mix.

Audience

Whenever I pick up a book that attempts to tackle issues as complicated as race, I always wonder who the author thinks will be reading it. Yes, like any author, I am striving to reach as broad an audience as possible, but I am also realistic about my context and clear in my intent. To articulate who I hope will pick up this book and take a read: I imagine it being those who find themselves living in the tension between intellectual pursuit and passionate action.

Neither brilliant cultural academics nor passionate social activists will be fully satisfied with this book. As I said before, I see this book as more of a dining-room table around which we can gather, rather than as a university classroom or a political rally. Again, those are wonderful and vital locations for learning and social change, but neither is the ideal setting for what I hope to accomplish in this book.

When trying to address such complex issues as race, too often we value one approach over the other, when what we really need to do is to engage both our hearts and our minds in the process. This middle ground is where most of us live and interact on a daily basis.

My hope is that this book will provide a foundation upon which we may build better day-to-day conversations about race, which may in turn lead to more in-depth intellectual study or outward social action.

Context

I will expand on the other "others" later, but I firmly believe that, along with our class, gender, sexuality, and age, the racial reality that we each inhabit impacts how we view the world. Because of this, it is important for each of us to explore and name the particularities of our social, cultural, and racial characteristics and how these things impact how we engage in the conversation.

> "Well, what does hell does he know, he's a straight, Filipino, Christian liberal from San Francisco?"

So here it goes, me first:

I am Asian-American.

I am Filipino.

I am Chinese.

I am male. I am Northern Californian. I am San Franciscan. I am Christian.

I am a college-educated, middle-class,

progressive Democrat.

I am in my mid-forties, married for over 20 years and the father of three girls.

I am a coffee-drinking, motorcycle-riding, lifelong Oakland Athletics Baseball Club fan.

I am a Settlers of Catan player.

What am I not?

I am not White, female, poor, gay, Southern, uneducated, Black, Republican, divorced, Latino, First Nation, disabled, or Muslim.

There are many things that I am not.

I claim some of these social and cultural locations for two reasons: one, to let you know some of the lenses and filters through which I offer my thoughts, and two, to encourage you to do the same.

I realize this kind of disclosure only gives some people permission to dismiss pretty much everything I say from here on out: "Well, what does hell does he know, he's a straight, Filipino, Christian liberal from San Francisco?" But I hope others will find my invitation and encouragement to name and claim the complexities of your individual lives liberating. I hope it can allow just a sliver of vulnerability through which we can gain new insights about one another.

Postracial

Just before the completion of this book, Barack Obama was elected to a second term as president of the United States. Just as it had when he was first elected in 2008, during the campaign, race conversations took center stage: Asian-Americans were lifted up as an up-and-coming voting bloc, the Republican Party failed to capture the support of the Latino

> *...in the announcement that he was elected, we felt that at least a few layers of historical injustice had been peeled back, releasing a mighty exhale of pure and unbridled joy. If only for a moment, a promise was fulfilled.*

community, and once again, for a few moments in time, many reveled in the fact that the United States indeed had a Black president. This time, though, there were no widespread declarations that the United States had somehow become postracial simply because we had a Black president. This stood in stark contrast to how people acted after his 2008 victory.

I still remember his election on that cool November evening. When the announcement rang out, "Barack Obama has been elected president of the United States of America!" I wept, I cheered, I prayed. Our world had changed. Our children's view of what constituted "American" changed forever. And his election didn't only make an impact in our country — perhaps arguably, the status and perception of the United States changed around the world. While Barack Obama was obviously not just a person of a specific racial designation, in the announcement that he was elected, we felt that at least a few layers of historical injustice had been peeled back, releasing a mighty exhale of pure and unbridled joy.

If only for a moment, a promise was fulfilled.

There was no such glee this time around, because there had been far too many incidents during the first four-year term to remind us that, while things may have been better that at other times in our history, we still had a long way to go as a world and society before we could, at any level, claim we had "solved" racism.

In the months leading up to the election, John Henry Sununu, a Republican and former governor of

New Hampshire, said in an interview that General Colin Powell, an African-American Republican, might be supporting Democrat, Barack Obama, because they were of the same race.[1] After actor Clint Eastwood's appearance at the 2012 Republican National Convention, where he spoke to an empty chair meant to represent President Obama[2], empty chairs were lynched in front yards in many parts of the country.[3] And Republican candidate Mitt Romney was caught on tape saying that it would have been easier for him to win the election if his parents were Latino.[4]

No, we still have a long way to go. In fact, with a far-too-long list of recent episodes, some might argue that the state of race relations worsened during President Obama's first four years. This is not what any of us had

---

[1] Lucy Madison, "Sununu suggests Colin Powell's Obama endorsement racially driven," *CBS News*, October 26, 2012, http://www.cbsnews.com/8301-34222_162-57541013/sununu-suggests-colin-powells-obama-endorsement-racially-driven/.

[2] "Clint Eastwood at the 2012 Republican National Convention," *Wikipedia*, http://en.wikipedia.org/wiki/Clint_Eastwood_at_the_2012_Republican_National_Convention.

[3] Google image search for "obama hanging chair"

[4] Mojo New Team, "Full Transcript of the Secret Mitt Romney Video" *Mother Jones*, September 12, 2012, http://www.motherjones.com/politics/2012/09/full-transcript-mitt-romney-secret-video.

expected; at times, it seems like the sweet taste of hope for a new day in race relations in the United States has been replaced with the bitterness of unrealized dreams.

Now, please don't get me wrong, I am not building a case for us to give in to the confining cynicism of the world. I am sending out a call for wisdom and deliberation as we balance the ongoing racism that we continue to experience with a deep commitment to the belief that we, as a people, must and can do better.

The biggest concern I have right now is the ongoing proclamations that the new generation is somehow so past race that we no longer need institutional safeguards against systematic and institutional injustice. We would be foolish to begin to toss out the proverbial baby with the bathwater and claim that we have succeeded in defeating racism simply because we have elected an African-American president or because of some generational assessments about race that have punctuated the political discourse.

But before I get to the dangers of walking down the postracial path, I want to acknowledge that we are entering the age of a generation with a different — dare I say more refined and inherent — understanding and experience of race, in the United States and around the world. While we will always have to deal with issues of race with the emergence of each generation, I have great hope that with each passing one, the kind of work and the depth to which we must dive will become less of a burden on our national consciousness. Glimpses of this truth lie in a few observations about the burgeoning culture that has dramatically changed the way we understand issues of race and community.

When people are freed to explore and create, whether in technological, cultural, or political realms, amazing things can happen.

Technology and the Flattening World

With all the new ways that we can interact today, from social media platforms like Facebook, Twitter, and Pinterest to our ability to have actual conversations using services like Skype, Google Hangout, and Face Time, interactions between different racial groups are on the rise. This increased personal exposure to different cultures has enhanced our collective understanding of one another, broken down misconceptions, and alleviated fears that were often unfounded. Yes, I acknowledge that each of us can also point to interactions, race-based or not, that have not been altogether positive, but overall, further interaction between and exposure to people of differing racial backgrounds are necessary if society's race relations are to improve.

Open Source Technology

The belief driving open source, the idea behind Wikipedia, is that over time and with the input of many people, we will collectively determine the truth about any topic. To avoid developing skewed definitions, broad participation is required; the community has the ability to correct and police itself as the definition is being developed.

This is an evolved and nuanced version of the "cooler heads will prevail" way of thinking, and one that I am deeply committed to. I have seen this kind of discernment taking place in many communities, and when it happens — well, it is inspiring and encouraging. This open source way of living goes beyond strict methodology and rigid boundaries and finds its life and energy in adaptable, flexible, and equalized decision-making.

Population Shifts

Recent United States Census Bureau projections state that, by the year 2018, there will be no ethnic majority among people in the United States under the age of eighteen. By 2043, no ethnic group will make up a majority of the overall population. It is clear that sheer population percentages are a-changing.[5]

Combine this reality with the new ease of interactions that technology brings, and all of a sudden we find ourselves living in a multicultural United States at some point in every day. Whether or not we as individuals can actually deal with the increased pressures of cross-racial interactions has no bearing on the fact that, try as we might to prevent it, the United States will continue to become increasingly multiracial.

Yes, technology, numbers, and new ways of decision-making have made an impact and given good

---

[5] Michael Cooper, "Census Officials, Citing Increasing Diversity, Say U.S. Will Be a 'Plurality Nation.'" *New York Times*, December 12, 2012, http://www.nytimes.com/2012/12/13/us/us-will-have-no-ethnic-majority-census-finds.html.

reason to be optimistic about the future — but here is the caveat. In a vacuum and with a confined demographic that has truly embraced and experienced the above three areas, we might indeed be pretty darn close to not just getting beyond race, but joyfully embracing the complexity of race.

But we do not live in a vacuum.

The United States is still burdened with negative realities that are intrinsically tied to issues of race. Consider everything from the incarceration rate of African-American men and racial profiling of Middle Eastern people to seemingly harmless dalliances like the

I fear that the notion that the next generation is over race will be used as a tool to justify ongoing or prolonged situations of institutional racism.

Make Me Asian phone application. We must be as committed as ever to naming negative situations that are centered around race and have the courage to engage in conversations about them.

First off, there is no such thing as a cultural blank slate. Not everyone is playing the same game and has the same historical worldview as those who are redefining our cultural experience of race. I will touch upon this later, but the widespread belief that because of past movements around racial reconciliation everyone now has the exact same opportunities from birth has led to a rise in accusations of "reverse racism" and the idea that skin color no longer impacts your life and context. I reject this notion as one that ignores far too many instances where race does, in fact, play a role and positively and negatively impact individuals and the larger culture.

In fact, I fear that the notion that the next generation is over race will be used as a tool to justify ongoing or prolonged situations of institutional racism. Sure, if our institutional systems and society were predominately made up of people with a new worldview about race, maybe there would be some merit, but that is just not the case. For the most part, our cultural, religious, and political institutions are still made up of and led by those whom institutional safeguards were originally intended to monitor and protect from.

Secondly, corporate sin and institutional racism are real. For instance, as many celebrate the increase in women serving in the US congress, the glaring lack of people of color serving in elected offices is a stark reminder that there is much yet to do in this arena. And this truth goes beyond politics. African-American and Latino students were still greatly underrepresented among those admitted to college in 2012, many mainline Christian denominations are struggling with how to become more racially diverse, and it has been long accepted that the United States prison system is disproportionally populated by African-American males. Does this mean that these organizations are inherently racist? Not necessarily, but it is clear that there is something systematic going on that is creating barriers to people of color being more represented — or, in the case of our penal system, less so.

I am a firm believer in and encourager of open-source culture. When people are freed to explore and create, whether in technological, cultural, or political realms, amazing things can happen. That said, I am not willing to give up my belief in the ability for a body of well-intentioned people to unintentionally oppress those with less power or who live on the margins of society.

While I believe that we have better and more

noble intentions for ourselves and that we will most often choose a path of openness and compassion, I also believe that the evil that exists in the world, humanity's constant yearning for wealth, and our self-preservation instincts are just too strong for us to simply think we can or will ever be able to fully corporately self-regulate.

Privilege

As one who travels a great deal, I have achieved "status" on an airline carrier, which often translates into an upgrade in my seating, moving me from coach to first class. I'm not gonna lie, it's nice to sit in first class. And while I do not turn around to face the coach passengers from my extra-wide comfy seat, smile, and clink my real glass with my real utensils, it is difficult *not* to get used to the luxury and comfort of first class and begin to think that my seating arrangement is a birthright and deserved reward.

And while I tend to fancy myself above such petty things as airplane seating, I confess that, on some of my worst traveling days, I have given that look of privilege to someone who took "my" seat. It's the look that says, "Who is *that* guy and why did *he* get an upgrade and I didn't? Don't they know who I *am?* I want my upgrade. Wah! Wah! Wah!"

Privileged much? Why, yes, but I earned it.

Well, actually, while I may have flown many miles, I did not actually pay to be in first class. Now get in line like everyone else, Bruce.

Privilege is when we begin to believe that our particular version of the world and experience of reality is the norm. All that comes with that reality becomes expected and feels deserved, to the point where we forget that not everyone in the world is born with the same benefits in life.

> *When privilege relating to language, access, or setting is called into question, those who have occupied these preferred realities may feel like things are being taken away...*

The feeling of privilege takes many forms, from subtle ways in which people grow up and come to know things like vacations, Christmas gifts, and family, to institutional privilege that skews our expectations and experiences around educational and economic opportunities.

When privilege relating to language, access, or setting is called into question, those who have occupied these preferred realities may feel like things are being taken away, when in reality, their settings, which are only theirs because of circumstance, are being equalized and balanced with those of others.

A good example of this is the annual "War on Christmas" lamentation that seems to begin just after Halloween. While some see the taking down of Biblical text from courthouse walls or nativity scenes being removed from publicly funded parks as an attack on the Christian faith, I see this as an instance of being held accountable for privilege and privilege being reigned in. For so long, Christians simply assumed that the predominate narrative of the holiday season would be the Christian one, that *everyone* should be OK with the telling and should themselves also be gleefully retelling the story of the birth of Christ. Whether Christianity ever really had a lockdown on the meaning of Christmas is debatable, but clearly that is not the case today. So when this Christian narrative, which has held center stage for so long, is drawn back into alignment with the realities of our pluralistic population, some feel like an injustice is being afflicted upon Christianity and, by extension, Christians, when in fact things are simply becoming normalized and brought back into balance.

There are many other examples of privilege in my own life that I always try to keep in mind while we raise our own children to be aware of others around them who do not live such lives. Examples of privilege include widely available youth soccer leagues that teach young people about community and physical exercise, Internet access, which provides information and communication platforms, and simply being able to walk through a store or neighborhood without having suspicious glances cast your way.

It is important to remember that acknowledging privilege does not mean that the benefits gained are bad in themselves and thus must be done away with, or that while naming them we should feel guilty for being able to provide these things for our communities. No, our response to privilege in our lives should not be to throw our hands up and walk away in a huff because our stuff is being taken away, or to put our hands up to guard what we have with our lives so that our privileges are not taken away. It is should also not be to pretend that the reality of privilege, as complex and confusing as it may be, does not exist.

It does.

Our response, for the good of the larger society, should be to realize that not everyone has the same benefits in life so that we can be empathetic in our view of other communities, gracious in talking about how those of us with privilege are perceived, and — most importantly — to do all we can to lift up the larger community so that more people may experience and benefit from cultural, educational, and economic access and exposure.

In April 2013, on Twitter, a meme began in response to a Tumblr blog, "This Is Black Privilege," which claimed that to be Black in the United States today is a position of privilege and carries an advantage over people who are not Black.[6]

The response, as you could imagine, was swift

> *#Blackprivilege is people so concerned about the welfare of Black Africans that they fetishize images of poverty, war, and death."*

---

[6] Tracy Clayton, "Twitter Tackles 'Black Privilege,'" the *Root*, April 29, 2013, http://goo.gl/yOQOe.

and filled with a range of responses from dismissal to anger. On Twitter, however, using the hashtag #*blackprivilege*, many African-American folks began sharing more perspectives of the Black American experience.

And while I did not always agree with what was said or how it was said, I was moved by the emotions being shared, I was angered by the concepts made real, and I was challenged by my own actions that needed to be changed. I was glued to the tweets that kept rolling out, and time and again fought the urge to respond with some kind of, "But that's not me," or "But things aren't that bad for everyone," or even, "I'm sorry." It was more important for me to absorb the words and simply listen.

Here are a few of the tweets that I found powerful, from the amusing to the excruciating:[7]

"#blackprivilege is death by 1000 paper cuts. But don't get too angry, otherwise 'objective'white ppl will use your anger to discredit you.

"#BlackPrivilege is having White people move

---

[7] I have chosen not to include Twitter names. I share these not to highlight the indivudals, but to the issues that the tweets illustrate. I have also let stand all spelling and grammatical creativity.

away from your neighborhood so your children don't have to go to school with theirs."

"#blackprivilege is being called "girlfriend" by your white coworkers regardless of age or position."

"#blackprivilege is cops letting me go because I'm well spoken and telling me to stay in school!"

"#blackprivilege is when store clerks are so eager to help you, they stick around & stare at you for the entire duration of your visit! :D"

"#BlackPrivilege is being 5'6, 270 pounds and still have White people ask me if I got a basketball scholarship."

"#Blackprivilege is people so concerned about the welfare of Black Africans that they fetishize images of poverty, war, and death."

Again, the intent of the #blackprivilege hashtag is not to inspire conversations or invite response, but to share a lens through which so many of us do not see the world. These hashtags are fluid, but I would invite you to visit Twitter and search for *#blackprivilege*, and then simply read and absorb the stories shared.

Another tricky part of the privilege conversation is that factors other than race certainly impact people's experiences of the world and access to opportunities. Issues of class and gender are intertwined with those of race in most cases, as well as other personal attributes. We cannot simply talk about White privilege as we so often do and then stop there. We can start there, but in the end, no one person lives in the world seeing and being seen through a single lens. It is impacted by the lenses of race, physical ability, gender, class, body type, age, sexual orientation, etc. We are each complex individuals and our privilege must be handled accordingly.

Further complicating things is that we must also not operate under the assumption that, across the board, heterosexual White males have it all, because some White males in impoverished parts of our country might challenge the idea that they have any increased access to economic or educational opportunities. At the same time, we can't ignore the very real negative perceptions of other groups that come into play: African-Americans and educational achievement, Asian-Americans and physicality, and Latinos and citizenship status, for example. This sort of stereotype is rarely attached to the White community.

For as much as I acknowledge that class and socioeconomics have bound some pockets of the White American population, the subtle benefits that come from being White in the United States today are still just as real as they have been for generations.

I liken the conversation about racial privilege to that of what it means to be male in the United States. As a male, it could be easy for me to say, "I don't see you as a female. I just see you as a person," or, "Gender doesn't matter anymore — what is this big deal?" in order to avoid dealing with the sexist realities that still exist in today's world and deny the benefits that I inherently received as a male.

As a male today, I must not deny the presence of gender, because that would not only unintentionally perpetuate a reality that confines women to a context that is still male-centric, but it would also fail to embrace the many gifts that the women of the world bring to our collective existence. In other words, no matter how liberated, educated, and empathetic I may fancy myself, I will always live in the skin of a man and benefit from that reality. To avoid participating in ongoing systems or actions that negatively impact women, I must claim this reality and adjust my actions accordingly.

Taking all of the above-mentioned examples into account, it is also important to acknowledge that one of the inherent dangers of this conversation is that we can begin to categorize people too much, listing out their different attributes in order form a convenient privilege ranking and encourage the start of an "I'm less privileged than you!" competition. This is a great example of how we need to look at and take into account big-picture realities, but be flexible and nuanced enough in our thinking to know that these do not play out in the same way at every time, in every context, and for every individual

Undoubtedly, it is useful to look at data on how different populations are faring in education, economics, and other arenas, as this information helps inform policy and structure — but for the purpose of our conversation, we must be diligent in not letting them become distracting rather than helpful. In the end, just as conversations on race require a great deal of commitment and discipline, unpacking the realities of privilege requires each person to be reflective enough to acknowledge those places where privilege plays and has played a role in his or her life.

Language

By its very nature, language is limited. I am fully aware of this. No word or phrase will ever be able to completely capture a speaker's meaning; yet words and how we use them make a huge impact on groups' and individuals' wellbeing.

...every person has a deep and rich background by which they have been formed, and which in turn has helped developed the cultural narrative of the United States of America.

As I lay out how I will use some terms, I hope that folks will be able to understand my intent, wrestle with the language that I have chosen to use, and try to avoid letting different interpretations become insurmountable obstacles that will preclude them from diving fully into the topics and issues that I have chosen to explore.

By now, you have noticed that I have included no glossary or list of terms. Whenever we talk about such a complex issue such as race, it is natural and appropriate to raise definitional questions. What do I mean by "race," "culture," or "ethnicity?" And why am I describing people as "White" in juxtaposition with "people of color?" Do I mean to say that Caucasian/Anglo/European Americans are ghost-colored automatons, devoid of all melanin, cultural complexity, or ethnic identity? "Here we go again, White people are to blame and we can do no right in conversations about race."

Now, obviously I do not believe that White people are without culture, history, or ethnicity. While it may take a little more digging for some who have been in the United States for generations to locate the details of their history, I believe that every person has a deep and rich background by which they have been formed, and which in turn has helped developed the cultural narrative of the United States of America.

The problem with trying to define each and every term is that too often we get caught up in disagreements and semantics, which leave us unable to extricate ourselves from these tangled webs of linguistic and morphological debates.

In no way do I want to dismiss the important

work of finding common ground around language. I know that language is extremely important and powerful and must be examined with diligence and care. I will address some language-specific issues in the next section, but first, I will attempt to provide some very broad and general definitions and descriptors.

I will try as hard as possible to stick with the term "race." Because so many folks use "ethnicity," "culture" and "race" interchangeably, thus creating confusion, I will try to stick with "race" in most cases. While arguably a modern social construct, "race" is handy because it generally

...understanding the implications of one another's skin color is essential to achieving any level of racial understanding and reconciliation

encompasses both genetic background and sociological location: African-American, Asian-American, African, or Middle Eastern, for example.

And while I am on the topic of labels, as self-identification is important in personal interactions, I will use a variety of descriptors for racial groups, balancing oh so carefully on that thin line of "just because you say it, I can too." I am aiming to honor some of the historic

REYES-CHOW

and sociological terms that particular groups have used to name themselves: Asian-American, Latino, First Nation, and Black, for example.

Another couple of words that that need some clarification is "racist" and "racism." In very general terms, I see racism as that which justifies and reinforces the use of prejudice or privilege in order to maintain power, influence, or control over another group or individuals. And no, I do not believe racist behavior is confined to any one particular group.

Determining if an institutional situation has racist elements to it is difficult enough; it can be nearly impossible to see into a person's heart and soul in order to decide if he or she is racist. Yes, there are extreme cases where most reasonable people would agree that the "racist" tag may be applied, but I think that the "you are a racist" battle is too often a distraction from larger, more transformational issues. In other words, it is important to remember that you do not need to necessarily be "a racist" to say or do things that are inherently racist. In fact, I think most people are not racist at their core, but yet without malice do things that further marginalize people of color by their actions. For this reason, I will use this term sparingly, if at all, when describing individuals.

At a very basic level and for the intentions of this book, understanding the implications of one another's skin color is essential to achieving any level of racial understanding and reconciliation. We can unpack language – granted, a critical task in some contexts – until the proverbial cows come home, but as soon as we leave our safe bubbles of understanding and walk back into the world, skin color, with all of the complexities that accompany it, becomes a predominate lens through which we live and interact.

I realize that these brief explanations will leave many people wanting. However, I do not want to derail the intentions of this book or cause the unintended consequence of calcifying the conversation before it ever gets started. I trust that, despite an abbreviated and insufficient treatment of language, most people will be able to navigate the complexities of language without much trouble.

At the end of the day, if you are unable to be in a conversational setting where language is in flux and dependent upon the person or the times without wholly dismissing the entire conversation or holding the interaction hostage in order to find common terminology, you may want to stop reading.

Again, terms and definitions will be a constant source of tension and will always fall short, but I have faith that we can deal with nuanced and moving definitional targets and still arrive at a common place of understanding.

That's my story, my hope, and I'm sticking to it.

Faith

While this book is not specifically about or focused on communities of faith, it would be disingenuous for me not to acknowledge that my Christian faith has played a huge role in forming and framing my perspective on race in the United States. My home congregation, Trinity Presbyterian Church, in Stockton, California, was founded out of the Central Valley farmworker strikes of the 1950s when the Presbyterian Church chose to care for the Filipino workers; the same Presbyterian Church (USA) played a significant role in the civil rights movement of the 1960s; and today I give great credit to the many mentors, colleagues, and young people in the church who have continually stretched my understanding and experience of race.

But my faith and its impact on my understanding of race is not only episodic and historical, it is also deeply theological and spiritual. As a Christian—some might label me a mainline, progressive, or liberal Christian—I believe that my faith is one way that humanity connects to God and God's relationship with and hopes for humankind. My relationship and understanding of God, through my belief in Jesus Christ, is one of liberation,

> *I choose to believe that even in our worst moments of despair and struggle, regardless of the cause, there is always hope.*

grace, hope, and gratitude, and each of these impacts how I see and respond to race in the world.

I choose to believe that being created in the image of God includes being created as part of an amazing diversity of skin tones, sizes, personalities, and perspectives—all part of who God made us.

I choose to believe that people can be liberated both from institutions that bind and personal attitudes that marginalize.

I choose to believe that a posture of graciousness in the face of conflict is more powerful than a posture of fear or division.

I choose to believe that, in gratitude to God for the very breath I breathe, for what has been and what is to come, I must strive to be a just, compassionate, loving human being.

I choose to believe that even in our worst moments of despair and struggle, regardless of the cause, there is always hope.

These are the things that my church and my faith have taught me, and I am grateful.

Today, however, I also believe that the church that formed me has lost its way when dealing with issues of race. During the civil rights movement and in the prophetic words of the Reverend Dr. Martin Luther King, the church was front and center in the fight for racial justice and reconciliation. Dr. King's oft-spoken words, that "the most segregated hour of Christian America is eleven o'clock on Sunday morning," was a challenge to the church and our country, that all needed to acknowledge the realities of racism in our culture and in our congregations. This was in no way a gentle plea for inclusion, but instead was a direct challenge to White congregations to fight segregation in every aspect of their lives: in school, at work, and in church. It was with this posture of conviction and will that, in the United States, the church played a crucial role in massive cultural shifts around race.

One result of this rich legacy is that the church too often finds itself trapped in the vernacular and strategies of a generation past. We have failed to find new ways to deal with the nature of race and racism that manifests itself in very different ways. Where we used to be committed to leading and facilitating conversations about race and racism in this country, we have abdicated that space to others and have weakened the validity of our voices when it comes to creating space where conversations can be had with humility, compassion, and grace.

An example of a problem we have created is the way the leaders of the civil rights generation can perceive young people and their roles in conversations about race, now and in the future. With much respect to my elders who fought so hard for racial justice and reconciliation in the past, I fear that, too often, these same giants of the faith have also held onto power for far too long. This long-term hold on institutional influence and resources has resulted in many young people, out of respect, avoiding pushing on past systems and ways of going about justice work. Eventually the voices of the church in racial conversations sound like they are coming from the 1960s—indeed, the voices are still the voices of those who were there.

In a genuine attempt to rise to a higher understanding of humanity in the future, we end up dulling the vibrant diversity that God has already placed before us.

As a Generation Xer, I know that I am no longer one of the youngsters; if I care about the future voice of the church that speaks and acts a Christian faith fueled by a yearning for justice, a spirit of compassion, and a posture of righteous indignation, I must recognize the opportunities for new leaders to be brought forward. I must not resent their new ways of acting; I must not abandon my role in their lives—I must embrace it all with joy. Not an easy task, but one that I must accomplish if the church is to be a strong voice of racial harmony for generations to come.

One final note about faith is that, in response to racial or gender tensions, many Christians end up denying racial or gender aspects of the Creator and create a kind of homogeneity couched the belief that Christianity knows no color, rather than approach these questions with a perspective that lifts diversity up as an amazing expression of God's presence in the world.

The Bible passage I have heard most often brought into conversations about race comes from the letter to the Galatians, chapter 3, verse 28: "There is neither Jew nor Gentile, neither slave nor free, nor is there male and female, for you are all one in Christ Jesus" (Today's New International Version).

On a first read, this sounds great: "Everyone is the same." But much as it has the quote from Martin Luther King Jr. I mentioned earlier, the church has sanitized these words from the Bible in order to make them palatable for the very folks who need to be challenged by them. Just as MLK's quote was not some pastoral plea for more diverse worship, but a prophetic challenge directed at White churches so that they would see their complicity in segregation, this Galatians passage is not a gentle call for us to ignore that which divides us, but rather an instruction to take a hard look at those who control the divisions.

In the letter to the church in Galatia, the church was being taken to task because of how they wanted to determine people's entrance and acceptance into the faith community, the Body of Christ. Some wanted to make circumcision a requirement, meaning that only male, Jewish, free people would be able to able to fulfill this requirement. This letter challenged that requirement, pushing the Galatian church to

> ...the church must find ways to see this diversity as a gift that, when lived out well, can open societies up to living together in more magnificent ways, to seeing one another as God created us: diverse, beautiful, and holy.

understand that the Christian faith should not build up walls based on race or ethnicity (Jew or Gentile), economics (slave or free), or gender (male or female). These words were directed at people with power in the religious institution, both to challenge their understanding of the faith and to bring liberation in spirit and action to those who had been marginalized and oppressed. Yes, a powerful piece of scripture, but not in the ways that the church has traditionally read and heard them.

All of this goes to say that I understand Christians' urge to avoid being consumed by conflicts and conversations about racial division. Having these conversations is hard work and can lead to more conflict before whispers of reconciliation are heard. On the other hand, what happens too often when we subscribe a "We are no longer X" way of thinking is that we then default to whatever the dominate culture is at the current time and context and in the United States — that is, White. In a genuine attempt to rise to a higher understanding of humanity in the future, we end up dulling the vibrant diversity that God has already placed before us.

In the end, Christianity's role in conversations about race and racial diversity should not be to blot out, explain away, or deny the real struggles that occur when diverse communities attempt to function as a society; instead the church must find ways to see this diversity as a gift that, when lived out well, can open societies up to living together in more magnificent ways, to seeing one another as God created us: diverse, beautiful, and holy.

My hope is that this book will be helpful in secular circles, but also that my Christian faith and commitment to communities of faith will be clear. And while I do not use faith language throughout most of the book, the essence will easily be translated into faith contexts for those who claim faith as a guiding force in their lives.

Other Others

One of the most obvious and justified tensions created when taking on the subject of race is that each person lives in the overlap of so many aspects of the human condition. While we used to be confined to claim a few identities, now we are given permission to claim a multitude of realities. It is safe to say that issues of class, economics, gender, sexual orientation, geography, age, education, and physical ability, among other considerations, make the pursuit of racial understanding even more complex. There is simply a great number of ethnic populations located across a wide spectrum of increasingly complex lifestyles. Race is no longer the sole determining factor of each person's reality. And this begs the question, "Can we really talk about race without talking about these other factors?"

Obviously not, but I will try to get as close to doing so as possible so that we do not lose sight of the main focus of this book: race. I do not wish to dismiss the important realities and experiences of other others in our society; these conversations about race might model how we could have conversations about the many other human experiences.

In any interaction, layers upon layers must be peeled away in order to get to the heart of the relationship. It is my hope is that these conversations about race will inform not only the racial contexts of our relationships, but also the ways in which we go about having them in the first place. In the end, some folks may have the experience that gender, age, ability, or something else plays a more significant role in their lives than race. With this in mind, I hope that in the places where common experiences are revealed, folks will be encouraged to assume the same posture of risk-taking and interaction that I am proposing that we do for race.

Chapter 2

The Words
We Speak

No one likes to be the cause of group awkwardness and discomfort — and yet that is where I found myself, stuck smack-dab in the middle of Awkwardsville.

A few years ago I was asked to speak at a youth conference. I don't remember the theme. What I do remember is the first day, when I stood in front of one thousand plus young people — arguably one of the toughest crowds you can address.

I can handle this, I said to myself.

I'm hip, I said to myself.

What could go wrong? I asked myself.

And then it happened. During my opening remarks, as I was introducing myself, trying to build trust and start to focus their energy toward the theme at hand, I said something to the effect of, "Just like I used to do, I know that you come to these conferences to meet new people and hook up."

Now, back in the days when "cool" Bruce was a kid, "hook up" did not mean what it apparently means today. Back in my day, "hooking up" was meeting new people or physically gathering together with friends. Apparently for the kewl kidz today — known by pretty much everyone in the auditorium except me — to "hook up" now means to have noncommittal sex.

Yeah, not one of my brighter moments in working with you people.

Now get off my lawn.

Obviously I was not encouraging these young folks to hop in the sack, but without knowing it, I had spoken some words that were not helpful — and even deeply offensive to some present.

At some point we have all been there. We said

something that we later found out was not received in the way that we had intended, we learn something about our own thinking that needs to be corrected — or we hear someone else say something that brings the conversation to a screeching halt and we have to decide how to respond.

There are plenty of ways that we can respond when these things happen. We can stay silent, stew about the incidents, and allow resentment to build. We can get angry and return with words or actions as vigorous as those initially delivered. We can just let it go, brush it off, and allow the perpetrators to think all is well. We can wait for the perfect opportunity to deliver passive-aggressive zingers that just make us look bad. Or we can talk about why the statements or actions created such tension.

> At some point, regardless of our social location, each of us will indeed "pull a Bruce" and say something less than helpful to the building up of community. So with full knowledge of our own foibles, let us be gracious with one another on the journey.

For the long-term health of the community, I think we should step out on a limb and risk doing the latter: talk about things that have caused tension and discomfort. With this in mind, the next few sections will take on a few of these kinds of statements, words that have often created such discomfort and awkwardness.

At some point, regardless of our social location, each of us will indeed "pull a Bruce" and say something less than helpful to the building up of community. So with full knowledge of our own foibles, let us be gracious with one another on the journey.

Let's begin…

Chapter 3

"But I don't see you as Asian"

I don't see race. People tell me I'm White and I believe them, because...

— Stephen Colbert, the Colbert Report

The quote above precedes TV personality Stephen Colbert's ongoing bit, a stinging indictment of racial realities in the United States. He finishes off the statement with such commentary as,

"... police officers call me 'sir.'"

"... I've never been arrested in my foyer."

"... because I think we need to use racial profiling."

(Pleated Khakis Also Dead Giveaway)."

In this bit, by holding in tension things that White folks may actually think and say about the racial realities of others, Colbert challenges the idea that the world is anywhere near being color blind and even pushes on those who think that is something to pursue in the first place. Brilliant.

We have been taught for generations that "We are all humans," and at a certain level, I do believe that our common humanity anchors our existence together, but there are a few reasons why attempts to achieve "color-blindness" must be questioned.

No matter how hard we may try, we cannot ever separate ourselves from the lenses of our life experiences.

I understand the draw of being able to say that we simply see each person as just a person, devoid of the characteristics, perceived or real, that seem to create division. That said, the United States and our humanity being what they are, I'm not convinced that the "true person" that we are trying to get to will not simply be an ambiguous White European-American norm that continues to define the overarching culture here.

I would also challenge this need to get to some pure humanity because to do so implies that we can — or should — get beyond our particular lenses to reach some place of perceived objectivity. This constant attempt to get to the "true" meaning of anything, including a person's humanity, feels like some kind of hangover from the enlightenment, when we began to believe that intellect and reason should and could trump all things. I do not find this possible, desirable, or helpful.

No matter how hard we may try, we cannot ever separate ourselves from the lenses of our life experiences. Yes, we can step back in order to gain perspective — but, in my case for example, as well-meaning and liberated as I would like to think myself, I can never truly see and experience the world as anything but a heterosexual, Asian-American male. These are not negative traits in and of themselves, but precisely when I begin to think that I am somehow beyond my own heterosexual, male Asian-American-ness, I run the risk of failing to take in account the experiences of those who are different than me. Because I will naturally default to what I need, want, and know, I can easily and unwittingly reinforce and perpetuate a culture or climate that is built around those realities. Those cultural norms, based on my world, are then institutionalized to the detriment and exclusion of those who experience a life different than mine.

A good example of this is the way I use technology and social media. Yes, it would be a little easier to shed my online presence than my Asianness, but my assumptions based on either identity can create the same kinds of situations if I am not thoughtful.

I live in a superconnected San Francisco Bay area where most coffee houses have free Wi-Fi,

> *Striving to avoid exclusion and discrimination based on skin color is a noble endeavor. However, in that pursuit it is also important to gain a nuanced understanding of color, race, and ethnicity.*

and I work with individuals and communities to develop social media strategies. If I am not careful, I might begin to believe that this is the norm and the way that everyone lives and communicates. Again, technology is not bad in itself, but when not everyone has the same kind of access, resources, or opportunities that I have, the way I set up an event or share information could unintentionally leave people out. This results in a cycle where people with a different experience are left on the outside.

Another challenge that I would raise has to do with whose idea was it anyway for others to *not* see me as Asian? On more than one occasion, someone has said with the best of intentions, "Bruce, I do not see you as Asian. I see you as a human being." Umm, I never asked you *not* to see my Asianness. In fact, when you say this to me, you are saying that a significant part of who I am — my family's immigrant history, the nuances of my Filipino and Chinese cultures, my experience of being a person of color in the United States, the complexities of being an Asian-American male — does not exist in your eyes. So what we are then left with is some vague version of Bruce... and I am not really sure who that person is. No, I am not *only* those things that have to do with my race, I also have my personality and other attributes, but I am nowhere near the same person if you choose not to factor in the Asian parts of who I am.

So, if you have ever occupied this "I don't see you as Asian" space, here is what I would ask of you: please *do* see that I am Asian and take the time to explore the nuances of that reality. This is not permission to default to lazy stereotypes (see the "Do you know martial arts?" chapter), but an opportunity to expand your understanding of the human experience, both through my eyes as well as through the rich and deep Asian-American history in the United States. By taking this opportunity, people will see how each of us sits in multiple locations, each historically and currently impacting the lives of others. Most people of color in the United States, I dare say, do this work every day, as we navigate the institutions and communities where, in number or in culture, the historical and current narrative is not ours.

Lastly — and this final point may be the most important thing that we must understand about race and how we see people — there is a *huge* difference between judging a person's worth or making institutional decisions based on race and understanding that race and ethnicity are important, real aspects of the human condition that must be and can be incorporated as we grow and thrive as a community of people.

Sometimes having insight into people's different experiences will not only make you more aware of those actions that may create negative situations, but also help you see the possibilities of what different people may bring to the table, broadening our understanding and experience of community.

For instance, when I work with African-American young people, I strive not to treat them any differently than I would any other students simply because they are Black. At the same time, knowing that their reality as Black people in the United States is different than my reality helps me to see the world more honestly. Knowing that many African-Americans have assumptions made about them in society — assumed criminal behavior, expected athletic prowess, or perceived educational failings — can help shape my own actions and inform how I can be part of tearing down those stereotypes. And at the same time, while I learn more about African-American history, culture, and tradition from those whom I work with and serve, I expand my own experience of the human family and can be transformed again in my own actions and assumptions.

Striving to avoid exclusion and discrimination based on skin color is a noble endeavor. However, in that pursuit it is also important to gain a nuanced understanding of color, race, and ethnicity. While navigating the world to gain this understanding might require more effort—it is hard work—if the end result is that we can truly see, know, and embrace the complex beauty of humanity that surrounds us, it is worth it.

Chapter 4

"No, where are you FROM?"

Place is an interesting thing.

I remember the first time someone said it and it was meant for me. I was in high school in the mid-1980s, and I was walking down the street near my high school. Some guy yelled out of a passing car, "Hey, Chink, go back to where you came from."

Cartoon double-take head-shake.

Did he mean Sam Brannan Middle School, the school that I attending before high school?

Maybe he meant my house on Roeder Way, from

which I had departed earlier that morning.

Did he mean Stockton, California, where I was born?

Ohhhhhhhhhh, I get it.

He was probably not talking about some actual place that I had an immediate geographic connection with, but some generic "anywhere but the United States." But that created another dilemma: did he want me to go back to China or the Philippines?

Maybe I should have asked him.

Now, I've seen enough movies where the smart-ass kid stands up the bully. Sure, the

> And while we often romanticize the immigrant journey, we also know that, as each group found their way here, they faced deep struggles, hardship, and rejection.

smart-ass kid makes a point, and the bully is made to look like an idiot—but the smart-ass kid always ends up stuffed in a locker, covered in some gooey substance, or left to clean up the contents of his backpack, which have been spread about the hall. Plus, after he humiliates the bully, the girl always walks away from him, glancing back with an "I thought you were different" look on her face.

I just kept on walking and did not spew anything back. I would like to think this was wisdom, but I think I was simply too livid to act.

As I shared in the introduction, this question of place and where people are "from" is frequently not asked in a mean spirit. It is simply that, like many other things that are said to people of color, especially those whose populations have a recent immigrant history, this is a loaded question.

As most of us know, the history of the United States is made of up complex stories of migration, both forced and voluntary. And while we often romanticize the immigrant journey, we also know that, as each group found their way here, they faced deep struggles, hardship, and rejection.

Those who were here before resent those who are coming now, and the closer you are to that immigrant experience, the more loaded is the question, "Where are you from?" Especially for Latino and Asian populations, the most recent immigrant populations, this question is rarely asked in order to find out hometown or geographic place in the United States. It's usually asked with a desire to find out the person's ethnic background—but when asked, it communicates, "You must not be from here."

There is an easy solution for this one. If you would like to know someone's ethnic background, ask them, "So, what's your ethnic background?" and if you want to know their hometown, ask them, "So what is your hometown?" But please don't ask, "Where are you from?"

Chapter 5

"If you would just stop talking about race, racism would go away"

Based on what I have learned in the past two decades from my work and life with organizations and individuals—oh, and being married for twenty-three years—I can assure you that *not* talking through conflicts, whether they be about race, gender, or who left the dirty dishes in the sink, is not a good idea. Sure, setting up straw men and trying to create conflict where there is none is also not healthy, but when it comes to race, I hope our culture will start to err on the side of talking too much rather than too little.

Anyone who has ever been in a relationship where conflict was present — yes, everyone's hand should be in the air — realizes that short-term avoidance is always easier than directly or expediently confronting conflict. Few people *like* conflict, and the urge to steer clear is a natural human survival response. That said, most of us also know, at least intellectually, that avoidance only generates unhealthy patterns of interaction and builds resentment over the long haul... and does nothing to manage the conflict. Additionally, conflicted situations left unchecked over a long period of time add to how difficult it is for individuals to extricate themselves from the system and often lead to drawn-out estrangement or permanent division.

In short, I have never come across people in a relationship in a stage of conflict who said, "Wow, that tension was never there until we talked about it." Folks may not have realized it was there, but believe me, it was there. I firmly believe that this holds true for issues of race in our culture.

Too many times to count, I have met with couples or coworkers after a blowup, and almost across the board, the blowup was founded on longstanding resentments over large and small incidents. I have also noticed that simply talking about the fact there was a conflict is a huge step toward releasing some of the tension, thus allowing conversations about the heart of the conflict to be had with a posture of openness.

On the other hand, I have also seen where the "Let's talk about this now, *right now!*" tactic has backfired because organizations or individuals failed to remember that not everyone engages in self-disclosure, self-reflection, and sharing in the same way. Some folks need to immediately vent their feelings and process solutions out loud, while others need time to process inwardly before being able to share feelings or contribute to possible solutions.

The personal nature of race, however, when it comes to one-on-one or group dynamics makes it imperative to create the right setting, timing, and process.

When these interactions prove unhelpful, not only is the original conflict still present, but there is a new and additional layer that must be also be dealt with. Basically, not all conversations are created equal, so when taking on conflicts about race, these conversations can't just consist of talking, but must be about finding better ways to engage in that talking.

As I have said, the topic of race is worthy of a variety of responses and places of interaction. Sometimes these might take place via passionate, public confrontations, as in a march or protest, and at other times, what is required is a measured intellectual discourse in a classroom setting. The personal nature of race, however, when it comes to one-on-one or group dynamics makes it imperative to create the right setting, timing, and process.

For instance, if I were leading a group through a difficult incident where some racial slurs were uttered during a confrontation, I would be sure to find a way to have constructive conversations about why it happened, what could be done, and then how to avoid patterns from developing. All people involved should be part of the conversations, and everyone should be given room to both vent emotions as well as seek solutions. Conversations should be had in a location where and a time when all parties can feel like their voices will be heard and conversations should be facilitated by a neutral party. When responding to these kinds of conflicts, you cannot take any aspect of the process lightly, for taking care goes a long way toward communicating a genuine desire to mend bridges.

Too often, in the name of expedience, organizations brush aside these types of incidents and react without thinking about the long-term implications or morale, thus undermining the long-term health of all involved. Conflict avoidance manifests itself in responses like vilifying the reporters, making someone "take the fall" for the good of the group, and justifying the incident—all which only build up resentment and, again, buy into the idea that if we don't talk about it, it's not happening.

In short, talk, people. Just talk.

Chapter 6

"Race is only a social construct"

Many years ago, at a different youth conference, the conference leadership asked me to help gather the kids of color in order to check in with them and see how things were going. The event participants were overwhelmingly White, maybe 95 percent, so the organizers were being sensitive to the fact that some of the kids of color might be in need of a place to process the experience.

As we gathered together, we had the young people introduce themselves, sharing with the group where they were from and their self-identified ethnic background. As we went around the circle, I sensed a great sense of relief from some of the young people as they shared their information. In the midst of a conference where they were often made to feel as if they were on display, like when the topic was racial diversity at a nearly all-White conference, in this room they did not seem to be the "only one."

Eventually we got to a young man who looked Asian. I remembered seeing him earlier in the week and inviting him to the group. At that time, he seemed a little unsure why I was asking. I would soon find out why. With a bit of a Southern drawl he began, "My name is Niles, I am from Black Mountain, North Carolina, and I am White."

Huh?

My inside voice was alternating back and forth between snarky Bruce: "Um, except that you aren't," and pastoral Bruce: "Wow, how are we going to help this kid work through this understanding of self?"

You see, Niles, adopted from Korea by White parents from North Carolina, for all intents and purposes, had lived his life as a Southern White young man. As I have continued to speak to Niles over the years, he has shared with me that that *was* his reality; in many ways he was culturally White. That's what he knew, that's the cultural location in which he grew up, and I have no doubt that those in his very small community did, in fact, see him as White... just like everyone else.

So when people say to me that race is only a social construct, a result of modernity and humanity's need to separate and divide, I do not doubt that there is some truth in

...when laying the groundwork for definitions and exploring high-level sociological developments, we must be able to navigate the gray areas and tensions between sociological examination and personal experience.

that. That said, in many cases, the "race is just a social construct" argument is used as a conflict-avoidance tactic or to dismiss the realities of what someone else is experiencing. Sentiments like, "Why are you so bothered by what this person said or did? Race is just a social construct... " shift the burden of reaction to the person who has shared the story, and can been experienced as a second victimization based on race.

What must never be forgotten is that race is deeply personal, so in the noble attempt to build common understandings and definitions, if the process of agreement or the understandings themselves are too narrow in scope, well-intentioned interactions may have the unintended result of stunting conversation and creating more feelings of exclusion and distance.

Imagine a child who comes to a teacher to report being called a "slanty-eyed Chinaman" by another student on the playground. The situation would be traumatic enough in itself, but to then be told that she should not be upset because the phrase "slanty-eyed Chinaman" is only words? There may indeed come a time and place to help this child think about the sociological implications of racial slurs — but it is not on the spot. When we inject the "social construct" argument at the wrong time, we discount the reactions and feelings that someone is attempting to articulate.

While we should avoid using the social construct argument as an immediate response, I do believe that we, as a culture and a society, must dive deeply into the root causes and political evolution of race in the United States. When groups of people take the time to delve into the beginnings of racial tension, it develops broader general thinking, which in turn helps individuals build a framework for personal interaction.

As we engage in these kinds of conversations and begin diving into definitions and semantics, let me affirm that are no right or wrong answers. Instead, there are different ways to approach uncovering what we each mean or assume when talking about race. There are, however, a few things to consider that might help you avoid unintentional conflict and tensions.

The first thing to remember is that talking about race in the abstract is not possible for all people. This has to do not only with rhetorical capacity and willingness, but also with a person's racial location. To ask an African-American to remove herself from the experience of being African-American in order to talk about race as an abstract and objective reality may not always be possible. The ability to do this, or even wanting to do this, is an example of a privilege enjoyed by those for whom the default objective racial norm is their own.

I have often found myself in conversations about race that make my head hurt, and not in a good way. I do not hold an earned doctoral degree[8]; I also do not lecture on race in academic settings, so when these conversations head too far down the intellectual vernacular path, I begin to check out. Conversations about the social construct of race, but which are not held in a classroom setting, must value the different ways people express their thinking and experiences and avoid defaulting to the narrative of those who are better at articulating intellectual thought. If the purpose is to gain understanding *and* build relationships, then multiple forms and structures of communication must be incorporated.

In the end, when laying the groundwork for definitions and exploring high-level sociological developments, we must be able to navigate the gray areas and tensions between sociological examination and personal experience. When we can do this, more people can reach common ground in language about race — and eventually create better relationships around race.

---

[8] In 2012, I was awarded an honorary Doctor of Divinity degree from Austin College, in Sherman, Texas.

Chapter 7

"Don't be
so sensitive"

My middle daughter, Abby, is a soccer player. She has played since kindergarten. She is also the kid that we have to constantly ask to "stop kicking the ball in the house," as she is always dribbling some spherical item off of any and every surface she can—including off of unsuspecting sisters and parental units.

We love her passion and dedication, but seriously, after an hour of *thunk, thunk, thunk* against the wall, it gets old.

Abby is also really sensitive.

From an early age, she was always deeply intuitive and empathetic, to the point that we have never had to scold her or raise our voices when she was in trouble. One time we busted her *standing* on the counter—at the direction of her older sister, we later found out—poised to dig into the sugar jar. We just gave her a disappointed look, saying her name with a touch of disapproval, and she melted into a puddle of tears.

Oh, our sweet, sensitive Abby.

Recently, this girl came walking off the soccer field after the opposing team soundly crushed her middle school soccer team.

Abby was in tears.

We have never been the "you need to suck it up" kind of parents, but I will admit that there have been times when I pushed too hard to find out what was wrong just because I wanted to fix it. In such cases, I only made things worse. Shocking, I know.

But on that day, there I went again, and I began to talk to her about her ability take things in stride, especially as she was starting to play against older, more experienced players.

Without waiting for me to get too far into my

lecture, Abby said, "Dad, I am not crying because I am sad. I'm crying because I'm angry."

And then she added, "Lest anyone think I'm a sissy."

While I would love to think my need to have her stop being so "sensitive" was purely based in a desire to toughen my baby up, I found it was actually based in obliviousness to what she was feeling and why. What I had perceived as weakness and a disproportionate reaction to disappointment was instead her response to a deeply felt emotion manifesting itself through tears.

> *Sometimes, in the face of that which we feel is uncomfortable, all we need to do is listen.*

I really didn't need to do anything but let her be. Sure, she might have to deal with others reacting to her tears, but there was absolutely no need for me to fix her, to dismiss her reactions, or to try and make things better.

All I needed to do was listen.

In the same way, when discussing race, I know that when I am told — and I have been told — "Don't be so sensitive," the speaker is generally not delivering these words with my well-being in mind. People usually issue this statement because they can't handle your reaction or because your reaction has created uncomfortable tension in the room.

When we respond thus to a genuine reaction, whether that reaction be anger, fear, or sadness, we are essentially saying to that person, "Emotions bad. Emotions uncomfortable. Please stop."

I can just about guarantee that responding to someone who is reacting negatively to a racial incident by saying, "Don't be so sensitive," will not lessen the tension in the room. It is far more likely that this response will increase tension — and in the end, it does not "fix" anything. In fact, what this response does is communicate the idea that someone's reaction is not valid and their concerns about the heart of the matter are probably not going not be heard. Yes, there may be a time to discuss and even challenge people's assumptions, but to respond with "Don't be so sensitive" in the moment will result in feelings of resentment, distrust, and further distance.

Sometimes, in the face of that which we feel is uncomfortable, all we need to do is listen.

Chapter 8

"Minorities can't be racist"

When we begin to talk about racism as an act, we are again reminded that things are very different than they were even a generation ago, both in how people have experienced racism as well as how folks talk about it.

One mode of thinking is that, because social and political institutions in the United States are still driven and grounded in White American culture, people who are not White are unable to truly have cultural or social power over White people, no matter what they do. This is an argument that is best had at an intellectual level, and when it is applied to some stages in our history, I am able to fully get behind this thinking. For instance, during the era of segregation in the South, regardless of what individuals believed or did, the structures in place did not allow Black Americans to enjoy the social or cultural power White Americans did.

But, like many people, I have broadened my understanding of racism and now see how racism can be inflicted upon pretty much anyone, depending on the context. Unlike a time in the early to mid–

> *As more and more races interact with greater frequency, deeply held negative beliefs about others based on race will undoubtedly begin to emerge in new ways in systems and institutions.*

twentieth century, when the dominant and public racial narrative in the United States was White and Black, today, the influx of Asian and Latino populations has created more opportunities where people of different racial experiences may interact. This is not to say that other race-based atrocities did not exist in our history — the Chinese Exclusion Act, First Nation massacres, and the Japanese internment come to mind — it is just that the conversations about race were dominated by the Black versus White narrative.

As more and more people of color begin to find economic and educational success and begin to climb ladders of achievement in both corporate and not-for-profit sectors, we are destined see an increasing number of power exchanges in which race will come into play. I have no doubt that most of these will yield more effective and aware workforces, but there will also be times when discrimination will come at the hands of people of color.

As an Asian-American, I know that White folks do not hold the corner on racism toward African-Americans. A family member once told me, when we were discussing interracial dating, that there was a Chinese saying, "The closer to gold, the closer to heaven," which means that the lighter the skin, the better. I don't know if that's a real Chinese saying, but it can be a real part of Chinese culture in the United States and reflect real views toward dark-skinned people: African-Americans, Filipinos, or Latinos, for example. And while this may only be one example of a personal belief system, this kind of public expression leads to actions marginalizing or holding power over other people because of race.

Some Chinese-Americans might accuse me of airing the family's dirty laundry here. So let me be clear that admitting that non-Whites can also engage in racist activities should in no way be construed as permission to paint Chinese culture as inherently racist or for White folks to now claim widespread discrimination. Rather, in this part of the conversation, we must remember the importance of being engaged in all levels of the conversations about racism in the United States.

As more and more races interact with greater frequency, deeply held negative beliefs about others based on race will undoubtedly begin to emerge in new ways in systems and institutions. We must examine the racism that manifests itself in instances of society-wide discrimination as well as the racism that may play into our day-to-day interactions. We must be open to the idea that, now, racism is not solely White people's problem.

Chapter 9

"It's not as bad as it used to be"

A few years ago, I was speaking at an event where John Lewis, the congressperson from Atlanta, was also speaking. I had the privilege of having lunch with him. No description would do justice to the life of John Lewis, but in short, he was a key leader during the civil rights movement, a member of the original Freedom Riders, friends with Reverend Dr. Martin Luther King, and one of many people who were brutally beaten by state troopers on Bloody Sunday in 1965, during a voting rights march in Selma, Alabama.

So, yes, meeting John Lewis was a big deal.

Little could be more memorable than meeting someone whom I have admired for years. This person had walked a journey through race and political activism that I could only imagine. Like so many before him, he put his very life on the line so that generations after could experience a fuller life in the United States. And now I was having lunch with him.

When we sat down together, I was relieved to find that he was exactly as he came off in his writing: humble, thoughtful, and passionate. But he was also genuinely interested in talking with a group of people considerably younger than him about politics, race, and the future of the United States.

This lunch took place in early January 2009, right after Barack Obama's first election and just a few weeks before his inauguration, so the momentous event was fresh in everyone's minds. The very first question that one of my tablemates, a young, local, African-American politician, asked was, "So, what's up with you initially supporting Hilary Clinton?" I didn't quite spit my water out midswallow, but I did think, "Well, nothing like starting with an easy one."

Without pause, clearly having been called out for not supporting Barack Obama from the outset, Congressman Lewis explained the process that he had gone through as he decided who to support. He initially supported the Clinton campaign and then eventually shifted his support to Obama. He spoke of this turbulent time in the life of the United States, his curiosity about how this new president would govern, and his genuine excitement about what was to come, not only for the United States, but also for African-Americans in light of the election.

He talked of new leadership styles, new experiences that were being brought to Washington, and the connections of the past to the present in terms of race. I never picked up any resentment about new leadership coming forth in Washington culture, he showed no arrogance because of his past accomplishments, and I sensed absolutely no fear of what might be next for him and this country in light of such changes.

This reaction was not surprising. After all, Congressman Lewis had been beaten nearly to death for his activism. I would have been shocked to find out that he was frightened of new shifts in Washington, DC, culture or personalities. Unfortunately, I have experienced quite the opposite from others among my elders, from whom I would expect the same kind of willingness to embrace change and to nurture it into maturity.

I have heard this "It's not as bad as it used to be" type of comment uttered in two distinctly different voices: those of old-school social justice folks beginning to see their power and influence power waning and those of young people who fail to see how past injustices around race connect and inform current struggles.

I do want to be careful as I level a blanket critique of my elders, for there are many who feel it is part of their job to lift up new leaders. I also do not at all wish to disparage or dismiss their role in the fight for justice that has taken place over decades in the United States: the struggles they have endured, the sacrifices they have made, and the care with which they have raised so many of us.

At the same time, there have been times when I have seen and heard young new leadership begin to step in, challenge current institutions, and again question the nature of racial equality in the United States — and more than once, those who came before, in what I can only guess is meant to put young people in their place, have dismissed these current challenges with a simple, "Oh, but it's so much better than it used to be." In other words, "What do you have to complain about? Back in my day, we had it really bad."

When I was a teenager, I was sitting with some mentors and challenging — maybe kind of whining about — the ways that young people were excluded from leadership in our denomination. Now, keep in mind, I was a young person at a

> *While statements about how it used to be are not racist in ways that we normally understand racism, when they are uttered, conversations about race become stagnant.*

leadership event, so it was not even that much about me. But the response I received: "It's not as bad as it used to be; you young folks will just have to wait your turn." It was said with a somewhat joking tone, but the message was sent loud and clear.

Now, for of us many whose elders went through very different experiences of racism in the United States in their workplaces, churches, and communities, it can difficult, if not impossible, to challenge their perspectives. It feels disrespectful to say, "Excuse me, but our time is now and you should be filled with joy that there are still young people interested in the church." Instead, what generally happens is that these young voices step aside; they defer to those who have held power and they remain silent. Eventually many give up and walk away from the very institutions that the generation prior fought to create a culture of inclusion in.

While statements about how it used to be are not racist in ways that we normally understand racism, when they are uttered, conversations about race become stagnant. Further, future generations are discouraged, rather than raised up, mentored, and given an opportunity to develop new ways of dealing with new forms of racial injustice. This almost guarantees that new forms of racism will become even more intricately woven into institutions and systems, because there is no one left to answer the call to examine and bring to light the unique experiences of people of color.

I see this happening a lot in the course of my

work in the church. As new communities emerge out of post-Evangelical and mainline protestant denominations, I have watched groups of people struggle with the issue of race. In a genuine hope to avoid offending one another or running the risk of causing conflict, these communities can unintentionally build systems that are inherently unfriendly to people of color at best and outright racist at worst. In addition to stating that at least things are getting better, they may resort to using the same arguments they use when someone comments on the blatant absence of racial diversity: "We invited them, but they didn't come." This says there is

> *The biggest problem with "It's not as bad as it used to be" is that we lull ourselves into believing that things are generally OK...*

nothing that we can do. They groups may plan events in locations that do not draw diverse participants, choose speakers who are predominately White, and rely on rampant tokenism. I do not believe that they would do any of these things with malicious intent, but the results are the same as they were for generations past: the systems and institutions are devoid of people of color.

Exacerbating this situation is another group:

young people. Not surprisingly, as they learn about historical racism, manifested in various forms like slavery, indentured servitude, and hateful legislation, when young people look around today, it is natural for them to think things like, "Yes, people are still racist, but is used to be so much worse," "Slavery is over and it wasn't even me who owned slaves," or, "Racism is over."

The biggest problem with "It's not as bad as it used to be" is that we lull ourselves into believing that things are generally OK because some of the most blatant laws institutionalizing segregation are gone, and because we do not hear much about lynching, cross burnings, and other forms of blatant racial violence. However, again, while we have certainly come a long way since the days of legalized slavery, we can point to numerous instances proving that both insidious institutional racism and racial violence are alive and well.

A good example of this is the way many Middle Eastern folks have had to live in the United States, especially since the 9/11 World Trade Center attacks. After the 2013 Boston Marathon bombings, many people called in false identifications of the suspects, usually describing people of color who were deemed Middle Eastern or connected to the Islamic faith. There were multiple reports of people being targeted and attacked because they appeared to be Middle Eastern, and online, the violence was evident, with many folks freely using pejorative terms such as "camel jockey, " "sand nigger," and "towel head" in their tweets. As it turned out, those responsible were most likely from Chechnya — distinctly not Middle Eastern.

So yes, in some ways things are better, but even still, they are not good enough for us to rest on the improvement and become calcified in our striving for racial understanding and healthy interaction.

At the risk of sounding like the metaphorical old man who lives down the street and waves his cane in the air, hollering at the neighborhood children, I want to challenge young people today to do two things as they enter conversations on race and try to fight racism in their generation. First, I hope young folks will embrace the past and hold onto the hope that the United States can achieve even greater racial harmony. And second, as they nurture this hope into being, I implore them not to abdicate their responsibility to monitor and respond to the ongoing racial discrimination that is going on around us all.

To facilitate this type of exploration and diligence in today's far different social and political climate, we must continue to ask questions like, Who holds power in our communities? What does this look like and why is this the case? Who has access to good education? How and why has this happened? How does race impact you every day in school, work, or in your town? Why?

Just as Congressman Lewis and others during the civil rights movement held deep hopes but engaged passionate actions, our current culture demands that we do the same — sit in the tension between having great hope for the future and wrestling through the realities of our current human division. For if we hold the past and the present in tension, across all generations, we can continue to positively impact the heart and soul of the United States when it comes to issues of race.

Chapter 10

"And out comes the race card"

A myth out there holds that it is easier to achieve in the United States if you are not White. I have heard it over and over again: "He wouldn't be here if he weren't Latino," or "She only got the position because she is Black." And while I will acknowledge the feeling, I challenge the truth of such statements.

You need only look at how key political, corporate, and educational lists are populated to see that it is not, in fact, easier to achieve in the United States if you are not White.

At of the beginning of the 113th Congress in 2013, the Senate was 93 percent White with seven people of color, and the House of Representative with 91 people of color out of 434 was about 80 percent White.[9]

A 2011 evaluation of the Fortune 500 CEO ranks revealed there were six African-Americans, seven Asian-Americans, and six Latinos — 2.6 percent of all Fortune 500 CEOs were non-White.[10]

Admission rates for African-Americans to top colleges are well below national population percentage numbers. In 2012, when African-Americans made up about 14 percent of the US population, only 3 percent of those admitted to Princeton were African-American, and 7 percent at The University of California, Berkeley.[11]

And one of the most compelling studies for me was a 2011 analysis of wealth gaps done by the Pew Research Center. It revealed, based on 2009 US

---

[9] Jody Brannon, "Congress Set to Continue Rise in Diversity," *National Journal*, March 6, 2013, http://goo.gl/zWlAa.

[10] "Where's the Diversity in Fortune 500 CEOs?" *Diversity Inc*, 2011, http://goo.gl/Lcmcw.

[11] Derek Thompson, "How America's Top Colleges Reflect (and Massively Distort) the Country's Racial Evolution," the *Atlantic*, January 23, 2013, http://www.theatlantic.com/national/archive/2013/01/how-americas-top-colleges-reflect-and-massively-distort-the-countrys-racial-evolution/267415.

government statistics, "The median wealth of white households is 20 times that of black households and 18 times that of Hispanic households."[12]

I lift these statistics up not as a justification or an attempt to make White people feel guilty, but simply as a way to challenge the idea that all you need to do is play some fictitious "race card" to make achievements come pouring forth. This is just not a reality that bears out.

While it might be the liberal, progressive thing to do to feel guilty for being White, I don't think it's a good idea to perpetuate a system where unqualified people are given power only because of the color of their skin.

I will say that that there are instances where individuals have brought up the issue of race knowing full well that it would distract from root problems or attract notoriety, but most of us do not operate at such public levels and must resist falling into the trap of issuing such declarations and forming assumptions about people or their

---

[12] Rakesh Kochhar, Richard Fry and Paul Taylor, "Wealth Gaps Rise to Record Highs Between Whites, Blacks, Hispanics," July 26, *Pew Research,* 2011, www.pewsocialtrends.org/2011/07/26/wealth-gaps-rise-to-record-highs-between-whites-blacks-hispanics.

achievements.

There are two issues that are raised when thinking about this idea of a race card — one being the White guilt, and the other, how we use labels to dismiss and distract.

First, I find it very interesting when my White friends admit to me that they have supported someone who they did not think was qualified, saying they did so anyway because the person was not White. My guess is that often a sense of guilt or fear accompanies that confession: guilt that they supported this person of color because that's what good, liberated White folks would do, or fear that if they didn't, some racial horde would be at their door with torches and pitchforks.

To this I say, please stop it.

While it might be the liberal, progressive thing to do to feel guilty for being White, I don't think it's a good idea to perpetuate a system where unqualified people are given power only because of the color of their skin. This only reinforces any negative stereotypes about incompetence that are too often attached to people of color. Also, there have indeed been instances of institutions and individuals being attacked by groups angry about real or perceived racial harms — such as the full media onslaught in response to racist comments, words, or actions — but the idea that you should somehow be scared of brown people is another myth that must not be reinforced or accepted.

The biggest problem with leveling the charge of "pulling out the race card" upon anyone is that it is an easy way to dismiss the gifts and talents that a person of color brings. Much like the phrase "politically correct" is often used to dismiss important questions of language and actions, implying that someone has used race as the sole entry point to a position of influence both devalues the worth of the person and reinforces the myth that I began with: that it is easier to achieve in the United States if you are not White.

While skin color and the perspective it allows is an important part of what people will bring to any endeavor, it is not the free ticket that some would describe it as, and we must move away from acting as if it were.

Chapter 11

"We need
at least one"

I know that I get invited to some events because I am a good speaker, because I can provide some helpful content, and because bonus: *I'm Asian-American.*

Do I get these invitations *only* because I am Asian-American? I certainly hope not. At the same time, I do know that many groups in and outside of the church are diligent in trying to create diverse experiences, so being a competent and known person who is also Asian is often a plus.

So while some will certainly think that other

people of color and I only get asked to speak, sit on committees, gain admittance to schools, or even get jobs solely because of the color of our skin, the places that take diversity seriously know that this is a short-sighted strategy that does not benefit either the institutions or the people.

That said, this is a common thought and driving factor for many groups who yearn and seek to have diverse and proportional representation. How do you achieve diversity without making someone into a "token" person of color?

Many would be surprised, but even having grown up and lived on the West Coast, it is not uncommon for me to be the only or one of few Asians in the room. This may occur for a variety of reasons, not all discriminatory, but when there is just one person of color in the room, problems of tokenism can arise.

Much like the "race card" claim, tokenism has the effect of dismissing the full nature of a person because he or she is minimized into "the Asian" or "the Latino" of the group. Many times I have been in a room when a topic arises that could use a different racial nuance. I say to myself, "Well, I *am* the brown person in the room.

Maybe I should say something." Almost inevitably, someone looks at me, maybe even involuntarily, with eyes that seem to say, "Um shouldn't you say something? In case you didn't notice it, you are the brown person in the room."

This sets the group up for three huge problems that come along with tokenism. One, the person of color accepts the title of Speaker for All People of Color. Two, the group in question abdicates its responsibility to reflect on how race will impact various situations, because now there is a qualified person to do that for them. Three, the token ultimately has no power to do anything despite all of this.

Addressing the first problem: no one person can speak for all other people in any particular group. This "I can speak for all my people" posture, which many people of color embrace because it is a way to gain power in predominately White groups, is impossible to succeed in. Since there is no way to fit every member of a group into rigid boxes, anyone claiming the ability to do so is behaving irresponsibly. Yes, as an Asian-American I can help a group to consider some broad characteristics and experiences of the Asian-American community, but I would never say, "The Asian-American community thinks..." because it is not possible to accurately complete that sentence.

The second problem that tokenism creates is when the body itself buys into the idea that one person can speak for all others in his or her population. "Great, since Bruce is here and thinks he can speak for all Asians, the rest of us don't have to worry about them." So often the motivation for seeking diversity is to gain differing voices, which is a good thing. But sometimes we include those speakers only as vehicles for our own protection; they are not being invited as actual people, but only because they are token Native or Latino people who can ensure that we don't do anything to offend Native or Latino people. And that's all they are good for.

This leads to the final problem with tokenism: when someone is tokenized, they are not given any true power, no matter how much they may try to gain access and give input. When an individual and a group both buy into the idea that a person's worth is solely based on skin color, even the most well-intentioned groups are setting up a situation where that person is not allowed to participate fully, creating an environment with no room for reflection or change, and ultimately sabotaging their goal of becoming more diverse.

When you are part of a group that is grappling with this very issue, it can feel like a no-win situation. And as long as we believe that having one person act as the voice of a group will solve our problems with racism, it will continue to remain a no-win situation. If the impact of a person's voice is limited according to their skin color, the possibilities for change become slim.

The best thing for groups to focus on when grappling with diversity and issues of representation is creating a space where people who bring different racial experiences are encouraged to share their stories — not just through the lens of their skin color, but from the fullness of their whole life. In others words, yes, we need to be aware of who is included, but we must remain open to the reality that *all* people bring perspectives that have been impacted by their racial realities, gender, education, economics, and so on. By setting such a space up, the group gives itself a better chance at becoming the type of racially diverse group it hoped to be when it originally extended the invitation.

Chapter 12

"Your English is really good"

The litmus test usually begin with, "Oh, you're Filipino?" followed by, "Do you speak the language?" Though this is sometimes asked by non-Filipinos, this question is usually posed by fellow Filipinos who are trying to see *how* Filipino I am.

For many Filipino-Americans, particularly those who are third generation, these words stab us in the heart, because many of us do *not* speak "the language."

The response when I am forced to answer, "I understand a few words, but no, I do not speak the language," is generally a slow, disappointed head shake and a simple "Oh." Which I feel can be translated into, "Oh, you're one of those Americanized ones. Your grandparents must be so ashamed."

Message received: You are not *really* Filipino.

And then there are those times when I have been told, "Your English is really good." And while my wife, who questions my use of creative linguistics, might disagree, the speakers are acting under the assumption that, because I am Asian-American, English is my second language.

> *We are so desperate for people to fit into nice, neat racial identity boxes that when someone doesn't fit in the box we have built, we don't know what to do.*

Welcome to my world.

I often wonder why anyone would even ask if I can speak another language in the first place, or at least why they would ask it so early in our interaction. I can only guess that, for many folks, brown skin in the United States means multilingual. After all, I can't remember the last time that I inquired into the language abilities of a White person unless our conversation was leading in that direction. I do know that some of my Southern friends get some grief because of their accents at times, but for the most part, White Americans do not have to deal with questions about their language.

Assumptions about language can frustrate other ethnic groups as well. When I polled friends in preparation for writing this book, a common theme was language. It is not uncommon for people to assume that all Latinos speak Spanish, that someone can sound Black, or that people are not legit unless they speak the language of their country of ancestry.

We are so desperate for people to fit into nice, neat racial identity boxes that when someone doesn't fit in the box we have built, we don't know what to do. And because language is such a vital part of how we experience one another, when someone doesn't immediately fit into our prescribed linguistic reality, our awkward response can be to question that person. We want to know why they do not fit into our understanding of how they should be: "How dare you act, speak, and live differently than I think your people should act, speak, and live?"

In the end, precisely because language is so

important, we must all be extra diligent in making sure that we do not take the easy path of assigning language characteristics to any person or population.

So if language is a topic that comes up, or if there is genuine interest and inquiry, questions and comments simply need to be phrased in a way that does not assume deviation from some abstract racial norm. For as is the case when you wish to inquire about other areas of a person's life, when you want to ask someone about their language abilities, it is not helpful to do so only seeking to affirm your preconceived notions about a person or a group. On the other hand, if your inquiry is about truly getting to know a person, and language may be an important element in this, healthy inquiry can help you build understanding and knowledge of each other.

Chapter 13

"You all look the same"

Sometimes your friends wind up starring in the best stories. A few years ago, during a worship service at the church I was serving at the time, my friend and colleague Leslie had one of those moments that every well-educated, kind, and thoughtful White person dreads.

This took place during the part of worship known as the "Passing of the Peace," While rich with theological significance, this ritual often turns into a raucous time of exchanging pleasantries and welcoming people to church.

On this particular day, there was an older Asian gentlemen sitting toward the back of the sanctuary. He had attended church a few times before, and he generally kind of kept to himself, but when it was time to pass the peace, he stood up and joined in.

As I made my way through the congregation, off to the side I heard Leslie saying, "Bill..."

Bill is my dad's name. "That's funny," I thought. "My dad isn't here today." Pause. "Uh oh."

Alert. Alert. Alert. Must save friend.

As stealthily as I could, I made a beeline toward Leslie, who was about to welcome this person who she thought was my dad with a handshake and what I could only imagine would be a hearty "Hi, Bill!"

As discreetly as I could and barely able to control my own laughter, I whispered to Leslie as I passed, "Not my dad, not my dad, not my dad." Just in the nick of time.

Leslie was mortified. Returning to her seat, shaking her head, she muttered, "Yeah, I'm *that* White girl."

Being the great friend that I am, of course I

laughed at *and* with her. Being even a better friend, I asked if I could share her story in this book.

And, Leslie, being the wonderful person that she is, and in the name of opening our dialogue on race, gave me permission. Thank you, Leslie.

Was there malice at the core of her misidentification? Of course not. Are some people just bad with faces? Sure. And does this happen to White folks too? Yes. But I am willing to bet that these instances of mistaken identity happen more often to people of color than to White people in the United States.

Now some would argue that this is simply an issue of familiarity and I am just looking for racism. Fair enough, but I would put forth that instances like this are also indicative of some greater racial realities in the United States and point again to the default variable used by most people when initially encountering other human beings: skin color and race.

While this might not be a huge deal to many folks, this "They all look the same" rhetoric has been one of *the* primary ways that society historically denied and dismissed people of color's human experience and expression. I have no doubt that every person is mistaken for someone else at some point in time, but I know too that my Black, Latino, and Asian friends out there can all list instance after instance after instance when they have been mistaken for a like-raced person who looked nothing like them.

I touch a little more upon this in my Bruce Lee adventures later, but here is an example. If I had a dollar for every time that someone said, "Hey, it's Bruce Lee" when they saw me coming, I would be a very wealthy man. Seriously, people, if anyone actually looked at Bruce Lee's measurements and build, the

> *We must be able to take the time to actually get to know each other in a way that does not dismiss each person's racial background, but allows us to appropriately incorporate our new understandings into our interactions with one another.*

comparisons would come to a screeching halt. But because this happens so often to me, it does provide some insight into the place where people start and then usually stop when first meeting me: my Asian face and an automatic connection to another Asian face.

I am not alone. My family watched a 2012

Olympic soccer match between the United States women's soccer team and North Korea. As we followed the Twitter stream, we began to see a disturbing trend — namely, "They all look alike" tweets.

"There is at least 6 sets of twins on this Korean team or they all just look alike."

"Does anyone else find it weird that all the Korean girl soccer players not only look alike, but all look like Bruce Lee."

"I think half of this Korean team served me food at the buffet I went to three days ago. Why do they all look the same?"

"I am not being racist, but all the girls on the Korean team have the same face. How do you tell them apart?"

Some justify these kinds of reactions by pointing to the idea that familiarity often helps people be able to recognize others, but the tone and nature of these kinds of tweets belied that. These were malicious and racist comments meant to demean. Period.

This plays out even in more personal areas of my life. It seems that at least a few times a year at gatherings for my denomination, I am mistaken for other Asian-

American leaders. Despite the fact that I look nothing like Rodger, Joey, Neal, or Kye, we are mistaken for one another over and over again, further illustrating the reality that many people really do think we all look alike.

Whenever this happens, innocently, as in Leslie's case, or with malice, as in the case of the tweets, I am reminded that there is still much work to do toward building better relationships between people of different racial backgrounds. We must be able to take the time to actually get to know each other in a way that does not dismiss each person's racial background, but allows us to appropriately incorporate our new understandings into our interactions with one another. This could be said for many aspects of our complex existence, but unless we are willing to see one another's humanity in a way that truly incorporates all the complexity, we will continue to be a people who find ourselves battling false and one-dimensional dichotomies of race, gender, sexuality, age, and ideology.

One of the wonderful things about my friend Leslie is that she did not try to dismiss, justify, or explain away her actions. She also did not get defensive or deny that what happened was problematic. She simply owned her actions and laughed a bit with a friend, and ultimately, I have no doubt that she will find herself engaging differently with folks in the future. We all make mistakes related to race, gender, or sexuality — or anything else — and this is the kind of posture and outcome that I wish we could all be part of.

So, if this happens to you, whether you are the maker of the mistake or you are mistaken for someone else — take it as a chance not to chastise or shame, but to seek or give forgiveness. Then get to know each another a little better so that it won't happen again next time.

Chapter 14

"Do you know martial arts?"

It never fails. At least once a year, during my travels, someone comes up to me and makes a joke that they think is clever. It might be a Bruce Lee or martial-arts reference, or it might be something about me playing the role of "grasshopper," made famous in the 1970s martial-arts TV show, *Kung Fu*. The real winners will either bow or do some kind of karate-chop motion complete with a mighty "Hiiieeeyaaa!"

Some people think this stuff never happens.

It does.

Now you might be thinking, "Well, duh, your name *is* Bruce and you *are* Asian. Seems fair." Sure, this train of thought *might* make sense if I were also ripped with muscles, had six-pack abs, were 30 pounds lighter and 2 inches taller, and could kill you with a one-inch punch to the heart.

Believe me, there are times I wish I could.

But no, not every Asian person knows martial arts or aced calculus in high school.

Not every Black person plays basketball or listens to hip-hop.

Not every Native American person...

> *If the intent of an interaction is to build community, we must take the time to get to know a person as the complex individual that he or she is... as we all are.*

Not every Latino person...

Some X folks may do Y, but not every X does Y.

When meeting new people or forced to make small talk with strangers, we can sometimes be confronted with an inability think of anything meaningful to say. It's tempting to default to what we first noticed about a person and choose topics in line with that, which we may see as relevant.

"What to talk about with this person? He looks Latino. It's the end of April. I know, I'll ask him about Cinco de Mayo."

Please don't.

Unless the conversation naturally heads toward a particular topic, comments like these show that the default point of connection or disconnection is skin color and indicate irresponsible assignment of general characteristics to every member of a particular population. Honestly, when it comes right down to it, it is a lazy way to build community because it reinforces and relies on worn-out stereotypes.

If the intent of an interaction is to build community, we must take the time to get to know a person as the complex individual that he or she is... as we all are. You may find out that the Chinese guy who just moved into town does indeed know martial arts, but you might also find out that he is an expert quilter or that he loves *Star Trek* or that he is secretly the fan club president for your favorite 1980s teen pop star.

When we take the time to get to know one another a little better and to genuinely take interest in each other's lives, who knows what we can learn about one another and how deeply connected our communities can be? The results will vary from person to person and interest to interest, but I know that we will find out more about one another if we take the time to take a deeper look than if we do not bother at all.

Chapter 15

"I don't mean to
be racist, but..."

Any comment that begins with "I don't mean to be..." is probably not going to end well.

"I don't mean to be a jerk, but... " signals that you are about to say something jerky; "I don't mean to be rude, but... " signals that you are about to be rude; and "I don't mean to be racist, but... "signals that the next few words will probably be, in fact, racist.

A few months ago, I stumbled upon a great twitter account, @yesyoureracist, that calls out people who preface a tweet with something like, "I don't mean to be racist, but… "

Here are just a few examples.

"i swear to god i am not racist but i am very thankful that my new neighbours are not Indian"

"Not a racist but Chinese folks — please stay away from getting behind the wheels. Your driving sucks BIG TIME!"

"Im friends with plenty of blacks. Just because i dont want my sister to date one does not mean i am racist"

"I'm not racist but if we didn't have a non-white president, foodstamps wouldn't be record high because they'd have jobs!"

"Not being racist but u know the incidents @ #bostonmarathon are by those filthy disgusting raghead bastards.

If you were to scroll through the responses to @yesyoureracist, you would see that many people respond with something like, "I can't be racist, I have Black friends," claim that it is unfair to call them out because they have free speech, and or try to justify their words in some other way.

Am I saying that people should no longer be

allowed to express what they are really feeling just because it is based on someone's skin color? Certainly not. I believe that folks must always be allowed to express themselves, no matter how much I may disagree with them or feel disdain for what they say. At the same time, I also think that people should have the integrity to recognize that some of their thoughts, no matter how much they want them not to be, are indeed racist. And most importantly, the freedom of speech that we are privileged to have here in the United States does not grant immunity from the repercussions and accountability issues

> *Free speech does not protect people from the consequences of their words; neither does merely claiming a reality make that reality true.*

that may arise as ramifications of our words.

Ultimately, the problem with statements like, "I'm not racist, but..." and the kind of thinking that accompanies them is that they create the illusion that attaching a disclaimer means there will be no consequences for what is being said, or that there is no justification for people to be upset by those words because the speaker said he or she is not racist.

Free speech does not protect people from the consequences of their words; neither does merely claiming a reality make that reality true. When we use the phrase "I'm not racist, but..." or hold the accompanying attitude, our words and actions participate in the widening of personal racial division and justify systematic and structural discrimination — which are built on racial stereotypes and assumptions.

In terms of reframing this perspective and thinking, I wish it were as easy as saying, "Just stop saying it." This is really not a comment that screams, "I want to be in community," but those who hold these ideas and yet seek to change must commit to taking a deep look into their own prejudices: why these feelings exist, why we justify them, and if they are something we really want to perpetuate and pass along.

And for those who have listened to statements like this, remember that this is also a great opportunity for you, to speak on behalf of targeted communities. You can bring light upon those who should know better and also show larger spheres of influence that this attitude is not acceptable.

Good luck.

Chapter 16

"He's a different kind of Black"

As I mentioned in the opening chapter about Lorenzo, I attended high school in Sacramento, California, in the mid-1980s. The community of my upbringing was middle-class, Asian-American, and suburban; the high school I attended was quite different culturally and socioeconomically, and decidedly more urban feeling.

Luther Burbank High School also had the reputation of being a place from which you might not emerge alive. The home of the mighty Trojans, for those of us outside of that community it was also known as Luther *Blood*bank High School, a name meant to reinforce the stereotypes and myths about that school and its community — none of them positive. I soon discovered that it was just a normal school for all intents and purposes, and I got really upset when I noticed it was often used as the geographic reference point for any local violence. Many reports started with something like, "A man was shot and killed a mile from Luther Burbank High School."

On the other hand, I had never thought that I was naïve or sheltered, but it didn't take too long for this Asian-American, middle-class kid from the suburban Greenhaven neighborhood to learn otherwise.

Those four years were transformative for me in so many ways, in terms of learning about economics, education, access, and family, but I was changed most by and through my friends in terms of issues of race. In a school that had no majority group, I sat with my White friends as they grappled with being White in a new reality; I begin to see how racism impacted people in deep ways, personally and institutionally; I was inspired by teachers and community leaders who were committed to teaching in this multiracial context; and I was forever transformed because I had friends of different races.

I have so many stories, and many will be saved for my "tell-all" memoir to be published after my children reach adulthood. However, one of the most significant lessons for me, quite honestly, related to the lives and experiences of the African-American community. Again, I was not totally oblivious to issues of race, as my family was deeply involved with politics and social movements — but while we fought for racial justice, especially for the African-American community, we didn't have all that many Black friends.

One of my best friends during this time was a guy named Craig. Along with Eric, Kevin, and Jason, Craig and I were part of a group that was a social experiment all on its own — we came from such diverse racial backgrounds and religious traditions and we leaned all over the place politically. We also dealt with all of the regular stuff that teenagers deal with: drama in our love lives, chaos in our families, yearning for success, cars, sports, drinking, and so on.

Again. Many stories.

At a certain point, all of my friends got to know my family. They were included in invitations to family gatherings and welcomed as "part of the family."

That said, I vividly remember talking with one particular member of my family about Craig, the only African-American member of our crew.

"I like your friend, Craig—he's not like other Blacks."

Are you kidding me?

Similar to cases when my emotions rose after stupid racist comments were directed at me, my first reaction was pure fury.

Craig was like a brother to me.

I can only imagine the person said this to affirm the choices I made with regard to friends, but it was ultimately a statement that disrespected my friend's community and justified acts of discrimination, exclusion, and violence.

"He's not like other Blacks."

How dare you.

While I would like to believe that things are different now, I lift this up because I know that this sentiment is alive and well today. We want to interact with people who fit into some category that we can label "safe" and "appropriate." We may couch it in justifications around economics, style of dress, musical tastes, or whatever else, but make no mistake: to hold this perspective is to insist upon interacting with the racial "other" on our terms.

We must remember that not only is it the prerogative of each community to define and describe its own reality, but that a common method of control used by dominant or majority populations has been to try and define what is acceptable behavior for a marginalized group before its members can gain acceptance and inclusion.

Yes, we can have larger discussions about what is acceptable in larger social contexts. For instance, there are appropriate contexts where we can talk and should talk about overarching First Nation, Latino, or Southeast Asian culture and how historic and cultural events and perspectives impact people's behavior today. These types of big-picture conversations about culture are an important part in developing understanding. That said, a "He's not like other Blacks" attitude will not develop common understandings of behavior; instead, it reinforces stereotypes, division, and the cultural status quo.

Of course, we cannot switch this attitude off like a light, but we can be deliberate in finding appropriate and meaningful ways to interact with people who are different than us and begin experience the diversity that exists within every group. I am not talking about looky-loo trips, where we visit a community different that our own as if "they" were merely specimens for us to observe. Merely walking through a neighborhood populated by people from a different culture, observing without establishing a personal connection, feels like a field trip to the cultural zoo, where people of privilege can watch communities in their natural habitats.

We must dive into experiences like my transformative time at a very different high school, so that our relationships can be deepened beyond cultural window dressings. Food, music, and dress are important, yes, but not ultimately transformational.

There are better ways to get to know people from different communities. You might frequent businesses in different parts of town so you can get to know the workers, patrons, and owners. It could be helpful to develop relationships with community leaders in different areas in order to build common understandings of issues they face and develop solutions that leverage influence and resources. Or perhaps you could just spend some time taking an honest inventory of your own divisive attitudes toward and unfounded stereotypes about other communities. Then, take all of these experiences and do your best to hold yourself accountable when negative thoughts and perceptions try to express themselves in unhelpful and unhealthy ways. Ideally, we can gain a fuller and more genuine understanding of the beautifully complex cultures that surround us.

Chapter 17

"It's not easy being White"

Throughout the writing process, friends and connections have shared stories of frustration and struggle based on being White. Now, few were crying, "Woe is me. Feel sorry for us"; they were expressing a genuine feeling of exclusion because of their being White in the United States today.

As previously stated, I am not White. And even though some of my best friends are White, I can only listen to their struggles and offer some thoughts and reflections. So while I may challenge some of the reasons *why* they may feel this way, I have no doubt that the feelings and struggles are real, and they are being voiced and expressed in more and more ways today.

Some of the questions and comments I have heard are: Why can there be a Black student union, but not a White one? Why do I have to pay for the sins of my ancestors? So much of this race stuff seems "politically correct." If I question anyone who is not White, I am called a racist.

However, what I really take issue with most is the idea that people of color are somehow being given a leg up... over and at the expense of White people.

A recent study on race by Michael I. Norton and Samuel R. Sommers from Tufts University's School of Arts and Sciences and Harvard Business School ended up titled, "Whites See Racism as a Zero-Sum Game That They Are Now Losing."[13]

According to the summary of the results:

> Although some have heralded recent
> political and cultural developments as

---

[13] Michael I. Norton and Samuel R. Sommers, "Whites Sees Racism as a Zero-Sum Game That They Are Now Losing," *Perspectives on Psychological Science* 6, no. 3 (May 2011), http://pps.sagepub.com/content/6/3/215

signaling the arrival of a postracial era in America, several legal and social controversies regarding "reverse racism" highlight Whites' increasing concern about anti-White bias. We show that this emerging belief reflects Whites' view of racism as a zero-sum game, such that decreases in perceived bias against Blacks over the past six decades are associated with increases in perceived bias against Whites — a relationship not observed in Blacks' perceptions. Moreover, these changes in Whites' conceptions of racism are extreme enough that Whites have now come to view anti-White bias as a bigger societal problem than anti-Black bias.

The fact that these feelings, perceptions, and experiences are out there raises a significant question for the United States as we experience racial population shifts. What do we do when a vital member of the community holds a perspective that is more perception that reality?

I realize it may feel like we have dipped into the

pool of the abstract, so here are a few examples of the aforementioned White experiences as I understand them.

When I was in seminary, back in the early 1990s, it was the first time that many people were seeing traditional language being challenged. The use of masculine imagery for God and the imagery that was used to describe good (White) and evil (Dark) were being reevaluated. The practice of studying primarily Western European theologians was being examined and called out as the church's reinforcing a predominately White male culture.

Some of the White males in my class pushed back, resulting in a number of awkward and tense moments in class. I can imagine that, with every mention of ceasing to study "dead White dudes" or suggestion that "he" and "him" should be balanced with feminine images of God, they felt as if their own existence as White males was being challenged. Frustrations with a White male theological and cultural bias were often delivered without kid gloves, so it is no surprise that some of my White male friends took all of this personally, going as far as to publish a newsletter extolling the importance of masculinity in the arena of theological education. But in fact what was going on was that their norms were being challenged, in language and status terms. The word and content playing fields were being leveled, so it felt as if something were being taken away. That couldn't have felt good, and I do not begrudge them their reactions and response.

So while I get how White people can feel that they have become the predominate targets of racism today, and there are certainly instances where White folks are pained and discriminated against because of their race, I do not believe that this perspective should be the driving force in our conversations on race. Yes, as we would for any human experiencing struggle, we must be compassionate and understanding in exploring the idea, but to allow this to be take center stage in conversations on race would be one more instance of a dominant culture being allowed to set the parameters of the engagement.

But do what *do* we do about the very real struggle that so many White folks are having around race in the United States?

One thing that we cannot do is dismiss the emotions of many White Americans or try to explain their experiences away. Much like my "Don't be so sensitive" section asserts, there are simply times where the only thing that we need to do is listen to one another. There are times when there is absolutely nothing to be said or done that will change someone's mind, and we must listen with care and build relationships of trust. In the future, at the appropriate time, in a helpful setting, feedback can be offered, reflection encouraged, and common understandings sought.

> *It is a natural human reaction to feel that, if we each hold a finite amount of resources, those resources must be protected at all costs—but if the resources we hold have roots in historic injustice and unearned privilege, protecting them will get us nowhere as a society.*

As racial relationships begin to equalize, in population numbers if not in institutional influence, there is a social understanding that if it is not that bad for brown people anymore, then it must be worse for White folks. However, this "If it's better for 'them,' then it must be worse for 'us'" mentality only exacerbates the lack of genuine racial harmony and assumes that the original distribution of wealth, influence, and access was equitable to begin with.

Now, in business circles, where the primary matrix of success and relationships is financial profitability, the concept of "If it's better for 'them,' then it must be worse for 'us'" may actually be true. There is a finite amount of resources available for people to attain and exploit. If the resources are finite, then they can be used up.

Back to my example around privilege and first-class seating, when I travel and board planes, I see that there are a limited number of seats in first class. There, if equal access and opportunity ever did level the playing field, a few of the people in the seats currently occupied by White men would have to walk a few more rows into coach, because they would have to make room for the women and brown folks moving on up. White men would no longer be able to be 90 percent of the first-class passengers.

The same goes for upper management of Fortune 500 companies and leadership of educational institutions and other places where White men still occupy most of the high-level seats. If there is going to be a better representation of people of color in corporate boardrooms, college campuses, and other places where there is currently a disproportionate representation of White folks and a limited number of spots, then inevitably there must be fewer White folks occupying those places. This shift would be, in the eyes of many, an indicator that our country was moving in a positive direction when it comes to race.

It is a natural human reaction to feel that, if we each hold a finite amount of resources, those resources must be protected at all costs — but if the resources we hold have roots in historic injustice and unearned privilege, protecting them will get us nowhere as a society. Thus it may indeed be true that as our country becomes more diverse, those who have traditionally held a disproportionate majority of positions of influence — in financial, political, and social realms — will see the scope of influence change. Honestly, it is no surprise and understandable that this shift would create tensions for those who see this as a loss.

What we cannot do in the face of change is to allow our instinctive posture of protectionism during scarcity to be transferred to our understanding of dignity, compassion, and community in our cultural relationships. We often treat our own ability to consider people as complex and created human beings like some kind of commodity that is doled out based on merit or availability, furthering the idea that if am going treat this person with a generous spirit, then I must have to take something away from someone else. And even worse, we can fall into the destructive trap of believing that if I see someone else being treated with a generous spirit, then something is being taken away from me.

> *Ultimately the question for the United States will be whether we will be able to see and encourage our changes as a positive development in an increasingly diverse country, or...*

While there are a finite number of seats in first class and at the CEO table, the same does not hold true for the larger experience of community in the United States. As our culture moves forward and race, gender, and sexuality norms shift and change, those who have held a dominant role *must* not act as if something were being taken away and thus they ought to move to protect it. In fact, society will only reach further into the possibility of a just and whole world if those who hold power and authority joyfully usher in distribution that provides for the wellbeing of all people.

So... all compassion to White friends and strangers for the emotional and physical struggles around your experiences of race, but the social understanding that racism is now worse for White folks than for others must be not only be shed, but challenged by you and by the rest of society if we are truly going to move forward to a place of genuine racial wholeness.

Ultimately the question for the United States will be whether we will be able to see and encourage our changes as a positive development in an increasingly diverse country, or if we will view them as the negative ramifications of this country's changing population and try to stop them from occurring at all levels. I choose to believe that we can get through the growing pains of change, and that we will all be stronger because of it.

.

Chapter 18

"What kind of Asian are you?"

During the 2012 National Football League season, on the show *First Take*, ESPN sports commentator Robert Parker made the following comment about the rookie starting quarterback for the Washington Redskins, Robert Griffin III: "Is he a brother, or is he a cornball brother?... He's not real. OK, he's black, he kind of does the thing, but he's not really down with the cause. He's not one of us. He's kind of black, but he's not really, like, the guy you want to hang out with because he's off to do something else."

Parker, himself African-American, was suspended by ESPN and then offered this heartfelt apology: "I blew it and I'm sincerely sorry. I completely understand how the issue of race in sports is a sensitive one and needs to be handled with great care. This past Thursday I failed to do that. I believe the intended topic is a worthy one. Robert's thoughts about being an African-American quarterback and the impact of his phenomenal success have been discussed in other media outlets, as well as among sports fans, particularly those in the African-American community."[14]

I believe that Parker was sincere in his apology but what he did was to bring to light an issue that takes place within all ethnic communities as they continue buy into the idea that there is a clearly delineated list of attributes that every group member must have in order to be considered authentic and genuine.

Some of the most painful examples of how marginalized groups can turn inward and devour themselves show up in this kind of ethnic verification

---

[14] Benjamin R. Freed, "ESPN Commentator Suspended Over RGIII Comments Offers Apology," *DCist*, December 19, 2012 http://goo.gl/l4dum.

banter. Arguably, creating division within oppressed and marginalized groups has always been the tactic of a dominant culture to keep those groups from organizing, but I suspect that this ethic litmus testing is also a natural human reaction when a population is not free to express itself in more complex ways. In either case, what we are left with are ethnic groups reinforcing the idea that their groups and the individuals that comprise them can be easily and rigidly defined.

> *...any population's experiences can be described in general terms, but that those descriptions are always going to be stretched and the set limits exceeded by the individual experiences of those who make up the group.*

I have been guilty of this many times. As I work with Asian-American groups, my work has often been focused on immigrant rights, just labor practices, and access to education, so when I see Asian-Americans who are ambivalent or who are fighting against me in these issues that impact Asians in the United States, sadly, I do want to question their Asianness.

However, if I am consistent in my belief that the

story of any ethnic group in the United States is defined by those who live it, no matter how I feel about my Asian-American sisters' and brothers' political or social choices, I must believe they are living and expressing a genuine version of what it means to be Asian-American. Believe me, there are times when I wish that those who wanted to publicly identify themselves as "Asian-American" would first have to take a test—*which I would get to write*—and only after achieving satisfactory marks on said test—*that I would get to grade*—would they be accepted into the club, shown the secret handshake, and receive an official, laminated "Asian-American membership card." Alas.

Another example—while we can loosely describe what it has meant and means to be Black in the United States, that does not mean that every Black person in the United States can fit within that narrative in order to be considered a Black American. This is not a new issue, but the debates have certainly expanded within the Black community in the face of growing numbers of Black immigrants from the Caribbean, Africa, and elsewhere. While the slave narrative can still impact their lives in important ways, by not growing up in the United States with its particular history, they may express their Black Americanness in different and sometimes contradictory ways. This kind of tension, which exists in all groups, though often kept "inside the family," can eventually manifest itself in situations like when Robert Parker questioned the legitimacy of Robert Griffin III's Blackness.

We all must learn to embrace the fact that any population's experiences can be described in general terms, but that those descriptions are always going to be stretched and the set limits exceeded by the individual experiences of those who make up the group.

Chapter 19

"But you never show up"

Acolleague once told me about a nearby, historically White church, who was starting what they were billing as a "multicultural worship service." A fine intention—which lost all legitimacy when they called my friend, the pastor of an actual multicultural church, to ask if they could send over some buses and "borrow" some of her members to help start the service.

You really cannot make this stuff up.

For generations, especially among liberal-leaning and historically White organizations, people of color have frequently been reduced to optional window dressing. If people of color show up, great, we will look ethnically diverse, but we're not going to try that hard to actually embrace and express that diversity.

Another example, one that is a little less outrageous than the church that wanted to borrow some brown folks might play out like this: an event is held or a group is gathered together, and there are few if any people of color in the mix. Someone, usually a person of color, brings this to the attention of the group, and after a moment of uncomfortably not making eye contact and hoping someone else will respond, one brave soul

> *No one really likes to be diversity window dressing.*

says, "Well, we invite them, but they never come."

While this may be true, this response is problematic for a few reasons. First, it shifts the responsibility for the lack of diversity onto those who would provide said diversity. It communicates that people of color must make groups more diverse rather than that the group itself might need to shift in order create a setting conducive to inviting, building, and nurturing racial diversity. Meanwhile, when this is the implied or explicit expectation, and people of color do actually show up, it is no surprise that they don't stay and these groups remain predominately White.

No one really likes to be diversity window dressing.

I am not sure that it would solve any problems, but what if predominately White groups copped the reality that some people of color may simply not feel welcomed by the groups' current manifestations? Doing this would force those groups to decide if this was a reality that they wished to continue.

> *Genuine diversity is not achieved with just a well-thought-out process or powerful articulation of hopes and dreams. Diversity that truly reflects the realities of the population as well as the openness of community might take a while and cannot be forced.*

Maybe more importantly, it would remove the responsibility for creating a diversity-friendly environment from those who provide the diversity, and return it to those who have come to see a more homogenous reality as the norm. Of course this is not an invitation for groups to legislate or codify systematic exclusion, but rather a plea for honesty about the realities of racial makeup, history, and responsibility for change.

On the other hand, many groups may genuinely want to find ways to reflect the diversity of the community but not know how to proceed. And though there is no twelve-step program to become racially diverse, there are some things that can help the process. First, have conversations about race and diversity: claim communal history, reflect on current practices, and dream about what might be. Once a community does this, it can name the obstacles to achieving those hopes. Identifying the potential stumbling blocks is vital; otherwise a community runs the danger of being surprised by obstacles during the journey. Next, try something that might help to shift the current cultural norms of the community, both in internal practices as well as in outward action. For instance, a church might try incorporating new worship styles or partnering with a new community group. And finally, people must be patient. Genuine diversity is not achieved with just a well-thought-out process or powerful articulation of hopes and dreams. Diversity that truly reflects the realities of the population as well as the openness of community might take a while and cannot be forced.

At the end of the day, a group that responds with any form of "but you never show up" must honestly decide if racial diversity is a priority and something that the body as a whole truly seeks. And while that diversity might take a long and difficult process of self-reflection, examining resources, and institutional change, getting to know one another as beautifully complex members of the human family should be worth the journey.

Chapter 20

"Why do you always sit together?"

In the movie *Mean Girls*, the new girl at the school, Cady, receives a tour of the cafeteria from her new friends, Janis and Damian. The "map" that they used was not one that would help locate the salad bar or the bathroom or show the fastest way to get back to homeroom; it was a map of social locations and the seating arrangements for the school's major cliques.

Janis: You got your freshmen, ROTC guys, preps, JV jocks, Asian nerds, cool Asians, varsity jocks, unfriendly black hotties, girls who eat their feelings, girls who don't eat anything, desperate wannabes, burnouts, sexually active band geeks. The greatest people you will ever meet, and the worst. Beware of plastics.[15]

Obviously this *Mean Girls* scene is a little over the top, but if you have been in a high school these days, it's not that much over the top. People sit with people with whom they find commonality, and for generations this has been true. The problems arise when those groups become exclusive in practice and purpose.

When I was in middle school, I was part of the Asian Culture Club (the ACC), and every year, someone would ask, "Can you be part of the ACC if you are not Asian?" and every year, we had to talk about what it meant to be part of a group that lifted up Asian-American culture but that was not about being exclusively Asian. As I think back on this, I realize that for middle-schoolers, that's quite the complex issue to comprehend.

Today, I constantly hear cries of reverse racism because White people can't have a White Culture Club, and in a vacuum, that would be a good point—but as I

---

[15] The "plastics" are the most popular, most shallow, and meanest of the cliques. Mark Waters (director), *Mean Girls*, April 30, 2004

have stated before, we do not live in a vacuum and can't leave because of or ignore the realities of race in today's society. What this challenge assumes is that the experience of White folks in the United States is exactly the same as that of people of color, but for a vast number of people today, this is not the case. Yes, there are some places where White folks live a "minority" life, but the overall United States culture still operates with the idea that the normative culture is White American.

While every group must be diligent in not becoming exclusive and unhealthy in practice and structure, I do believe that there are times when like-cultured people need to spend time together, just them.

I often travel to the Philippines, and there are communities gathered around language or country of origin there because they are in the minority. An English-speaking group would be appropriate in the Philippines, because the dominant language is Tagalog or another dialect. There would be no reason to have a Filipino Culture Club, because that is the dominant cultural norm. People in the minority need groups such as this in order to find support and community. These groups are not in any way anti-Philippines or trying to create enclaves where people can hunker down and remain separate from the rest of the culture. On the contrary, the many English-speaking churches and other organizations help facilitate better integration into the culture.

In the United States, where White American culture dominates, many people of color, when entering a room of people, gathering at a conference, or even walking down the street, will feel an almost unspoken connection to other people of color. There is a commonality that may have been indirectly created in reaction to living in White culture, but it's more about acknowledging an unspoken and shared story and experience.

Yes, there are always exceptions, but in general, people — especially people of color — do not gather in the name of excluding White folks, but because there is familiarity and comfort in that space. In fact, when White friends point out that some group is always gathering together, I ask them how often they are in a room or gathering entirely consisting of White folks. The "oh yeah" that ensues is a good reminder that the lives and gatherings of people of color do not revolve around or base themselves upon the needs and comfort of White people, but their own.

While every group must be diligent in not becoming exclusive and unhealthy in practice and structure, I do believe that there are times when like-cultured people need to spend time together, just them. Sometimes gathering free of the people who represent those with whom past struggles occurred — whether they are directly responsible for those or not — can be a transformative time for exploration and

> *So if you ever fear that folks are gathering "without you," remind yourself that it might not actually be about you, but rather about the needs of the group.*

discovery. For instance, I consider myself a liberated male and I do not think that many of my female friends would hold back in their sharing because I was in the room. However, I have no doubt that, if a conversation were to be held about issues facing my female friends, their tone and language would be very different if I were in the room. There are definitely times for all parties to gather in one room for cross discussion, but there are also times when groups must gather on their own.

Now, hopefully obviously, I offer this idea not to inspire people to start pride groups of any hue. These groups are more interested in power and division than in getting at core issues of race and causes of racism. I offer this idea as a way to understand why these kinds of groups tend to come together naturally, and why, when they gather with intent, they can also bring great benefit and understanding to the conversations on race.

So if you ever fear that folks are gathering "without you," remind yourself that it might not actually be about you, but rather about the needs of the group. And because this is a reality that will not change, whether it's in the high school cafeteria, at the neighborhood dog park, or in the church down the street, shifting perspective about what is going on will help alleviate tension and discomfort.

Chapter 21

"Asian is in"

I have always been fascinated by people who get tattoos of Asian characters on their body. Assuming that the characters actually mean what the person thinks they mean, what is it about having "peace" or "water" tattooed on your body in a language that you cannot read? I am willing to bet that most folks who have Asian characters permanently tattooed on their bodies have them because they believe that there is something "cool" about the look of the words and not the words themselves. If this were not the case, there would be hordes of people walking around with English words like "water" or "calm" tattooed around their ankles. The epitome of using culture as an ornament, this is one way that we co-opt culture without any reason.

Another longtime culprit in the world of cultural commoditization is sports teams at all levels. The debate about the use of cultures as mascots has been going on for a long time. From the National Football League's Washington Redskins to Major League Baseball's Cleveland Indians and their mascot Chief Wahoo, those involved in professional sports have dealt with this tension for generations.

And it is still a current discussion.

In December 2012, Major League Baseball released the batting practice hat designs for the 2013 season. Most folks do not really like change, and when a sports team offers new designs, there is usually some grumbling and hankering for what has been. The Atlanta Braves unveiled the following hat design:

OLD   NEW

With the release of what is known as the "screaming Indian" or "screaming savage," the debate over the appropriate use of mascots and logos based on ethnic groups was once again ignited. The Atlanta Braves is not the only team to have been challenged for its use of what many see as caricatures and offensive; this has been going on for decades everywhere from high school to professional sports franchises.

To some, this debate over mascots is the ultimate example of political correctness run amok. For others, however, the return of the Atlanta Braves' "screaming savage"

> ...there is a fine line between expressing respect or honor for or solidarity with a population and romanticizing, exploiting, and co-opting its culture for personal or financial gain.

symbolizes where people of color in general, and Native Americans in particular, truly stand in the life and culture of the United States. The proponents of these kinds of mascots argue that their use shows respect and honor, so people should not only not be offended, but they should even be thankful that their cultures are being lifted up. Others say that these mascots only perpetuate a very narrow cultural example at best, and perpetuate outright racist thinking at worst. While there may be some mascots where the debate about legitimacy is valid, when it comes to the Braves, claiming that the baseball mascot is being used to honor and respect a culture when he is actually named Chief Noc-A-Homa, it's hard to take the respect and honor argument seriously.

Mascots are not the only place where culture and ethnicity have been leveraged and made visible in new ways and to new eyes. In many industries, including fashion, entertainment, and architecture, cultural influences show up both in positive and negative ways. To sample a culture is not in itself a bad thing, but there is a fine line between expressing respect or honor for or solidarity with a population and romanticizing, exploiting, and co-opting its culture for personal or financial gain.

There are no steadfast rules about how, when, or if cultural references should be used. In fact, I think it is generally a positive thing for more people to be exposed to more cultures and the complexities that they entail, but this must be driven by a genuine understanding of and inquiry into the culture. Cultural references and affirmation must not be only about clothing, music, food, or the above-mentioned tattoos — all of those can too easily be translated into one-dimensional caricatures of a people. Each step into another culture must be treated as an entry into a deeper knowledge and understanding of those things but also all other aspects of a population.

In the end, if it feels wrong and it seems like the cultural reference has become a mascot or costume, it probably is and should be discontinued.

Chapter 22

"If they can say it, why can't I?"

I wonder if there is a name for a specific occurrence in movies or television shows that feature African-Americans in a culture where the words "nigger" or "nigga" are bandied about. The occurrence I wonder about is that awkward moment in the show when someone who is *not* African-American decides that it's OK for him to use this language.

It goes something like this.

White guy enters room, lifts hand to give a high-five to the biggest and scariest-looking dude in the room, and says, "What's up my nigga?"

Awkward. Silence.

One of two things then happens: either the White guy's Black friend saves him from getting his ass kicked and being tossed out the backdoor into an alley, or the White guy gets his ass kicked and is tossed out the backdoor into an alley.

Putting aside the too-numerous-too-count stereotypes that often accompany such movies, I know some form of this situation must take place in real life.

I've seen it. Heck, I've probably been that guy.

> As a man who has three daughters and one wife, should it be OK for me to tell jokes about menstruation, giving birth, or vaginas? Nope.

It is hotly debated within the African-American community whether anyone should even use the word "nigga" as part of an accepted nomenclature. Some think it is a way to take power away from the word; others think that its usage only perpetuates blatant stereotypes about and negative self-imagery within the African-American community.

That is a debate well worth having—but no matter what I, an Asian-American, think about the debate, I must tread lightly if I want take part in any aspect of that conversation. I must be cautious that I don't allow myself to believe that I am so "cool" or accepted that I can assume inclusion in the African-American community. For no matter how much I may feel in solidarity with my African-American friends, I will never fully understand or feel the weight of what it means to be called a "nigger" or "nigga."

Never.

As a man, I will never fully feel the effect that being called a "slut," "whore," or "bitch" has upon women in the world.

Never.

And if you are not Asian, you will never understand what it is like to be called a "Chink," "gook" or "FOB" (meaning fresh off the boat) and then be told to go back to your own country.

Never.

With this in mind, in my family, we often remind our daughters that there are simply things that they can say and others should not as well as things that others can say, but that they cannot. On the outside and to those with a very rigid understanding of what is right or wrong, this is a difficult concept and feels like an unfair double standard. After all, if it is OK for that person to say something, why isn't it OK for me to say it?

As a man who has three daughters and one wife, should it be OK for me to tell jokes about menstruation, giving birth, or vaginas?

Nope.

If you talk bad about your family and the crazy dysfunction that drives you nuts, can I join in on the family bashing and criticize your mother?

Nope.

And if there are a bunch of Middle Eastern folks hanging out joking about how the world sees them, including references to bombs and terrorism, can I, as a non-Middle Eastern person, join in?

Again: nope.

Part of understanding this delicate and nuanced aspect of racial relations is to understand that part of using particular words within a community or family is, again, to take the power away from those words. I have heard these kinds of words referred to as "sadlarious," or words that cause us to "crylaugh."

I often explain to others that laughing about Asian-American stereotypes is a way for our community to deal with the pain and power that some of those stereotypes have held over us for generations: "We laugh so we don't cry," or "We laugh to mask the pain." So when people who are outside of the family try to join in, it's awkward, because those words do not carry the same weight or shared story, and the newcomer is giving power back to the words.

But what about the person who has been given "honorary" status by a racial community? What then?

This is a common occurrence in many communities, usually bestowed upon a White person who has proven his or her commitment to a community. He or she eats the foods of the people, lives in the same neighborhood, and genuinely lives the culture. In my experience, these are exactly the people who understand even more deeply the importance of knowing that, while they may have honorary Filipino status, for example, they can still never fully understand the experience of being Filipino.

Even my wife of twenty-three years, who is

White and has totally been given honorary Filipino status — they call her "Manang Robin," — often remarks, "And again, you can say that, I cannot," when our family begins to riff on Filipino culture, family dynamics, old-man accents, or the crazy foods we eat.

She gets it. Love that lady.

It is important to understand that, when talking about what you should or should not say in the context of conversations about race, it is never about trying to limit free speech or deny your right to speak your mind. No, when it comes to an area like this, it is about

> *It is important to remember that there are ramifications for the words we choose and the contexts in which we choose to use them. No word is spoken in a vacuum.*

understanding that words do not exist in a vacuum — the words that we use carry history for each of us. Some is good and some bad, but it's all there nonetheless.

When someone is struggling with this question, it is important to ask "Why do you *want* to use those terms?" and "To what end?" I suspect that, for the vast majority of people who think my explanation seems unfair, it is more about wanting to be included in a culture that is not their own instead of wanting a more genuine understanding of the experience of another racial group. This is not a negative inclination in itself, but it is simply unattainable.

My suggestion would be, unless you want to face a lifetime of frustration, to explore your own culture. This will help expose the breadth of our racial realities and in turn will help us appreciate the realities of other racial groups.

It is important to remember that there are ramifications for the words we choose and the contexts in which we choose to use them. No word is spoken in a vacuum, so responding to being called out for saying something racist with, "What? All I said was the same thing that she said," ignores the reality that while the words may be the same, when someone outside of the family says them, they in no way mean the same thing.

Chapter 23

"Those people..."

Running a close second to, "I am not racist, but..." in proclaiming that something unhelpful is about to be said is any statement that includes the words, "those people... "

Red. Flag. City.

Almost regardless of the context or intent, there is no way to escape the fact that using the phrase, "those people," sets the speaker up to make sweeping generalizations. It also communicates and assumes a distance and a divide between the targeted group and the one doing the targeting.

I saved this one for last, because out of all of the

statements that I have shared, this is probably the easiest to rectify. My advice: remove the phrase from your lexicon and never ever say it again.

Ever.

There are a myriad of other ways to rephrase statements that might require bringing attention to a particular group of people. A simple shift in words from "those" to "the" immediately removes the tone of "them... way over there," and simply names a group of people. The comment, "The people who just moved into the neighborhood are Latino," sounds very different than, "Those people who just moved into the neighborhood are Latino."

I realize that many folks have already erased this set of words from their mental phrase book, but I felt like I should mention it, just in case...

Chapter 24

This Isn't
the Last Word

My favorite book when I was growing up was a Sesame Street book starring blue-furred Grover: *The Monster at the End of This Book.* On each page, lovable, furry old Grover pleads with the reader not to turn the page, saying, "There is a monster at the end of this book!" With great fervor, he tries to stop us from turning the page again. But to avail, and despite Grover's pleas, the reader turns page after page after page, with each page moving us all closer to the end of the book and whatever menacing creature lies waiting for us there.

Like Grover, when tracking such immense conversations as race, it seems that too often we place too much emphasis on the end of a book, class, or study to result in something grand and great: a solution, a realization, a miracle. It should be no surprise that this was never my intent. Just as Grover discovered that the monster end of the book was just him—lovable, furry old Grover and not a big menacing figure—I hope that we can all grasp that at the end of the book and the end of the day, it is just us left. Just us, still trying to figure out how to live together a little bit better on the next page of our lives than we did on the prior pages.

> ...we, *as a people and a culture, have shown over time that when thoughtful people speak and act with care, we can make it to the other side of the struggle better for the journey.*

This journey that we take together around race must not be undertaken with such urgency that it winds up making us think there is some endpoint that we'll have to reach in order to be successful. Like any journey in life, as we each commit to entering conversations on race, there will be ebbs and flows of energy.

We'll have reasons to celebrate and there will be disappointments; and we may even make mistakes more often than we get it right. The important thing to remember is that we, as a people and a culture, have shown over time that when thoughtful people speak and act with care, we can make it to the other side of the struggle better for the journey. Each generation must discover the divides that it needs to cross, and as our collective journey unfolds, I hope this book and the conversations it inspires will be helpful companions along the way.

So, as you finish this book, I want to tell you that I deeply appreciate your taking this journey with me. I hope you found something that was challenging, inspiring, and ultimately helpful as you live out community in this wonderfully and beautifully complex world.

May you find the space, courage, and hope to curate your own conversations about race, today and tomorrow.

Peace.

Roll Credits

To those of you who like to sit through the very end of the movie: this is your section. Here is a little information about the entire book process, a few final thank yous to the many folks who have been part of this journey, and some resources and goodies that I think folks may find helpful.

Please remember to deposit your trash in the appropriate receptacle as you leave the theater. ☺

Behind the Scenes

One of my favorite shows when I was growing up was *Behind the Music* on VH-1. Each episode would feature a different celebrity, who would give a brief glimpse into his or her life and what made him or her tick. I have always been the kind of person who wonders, "Why did she do this or that?" or "There must be more to the story, right?" If you are like that too, here is a little more background about the whys, whens, and hows that gave birth to this book project.

It all began way, way, way back in September 2012—yes, only about ten months prior to the actual release of *But I don't see you as Asian*. I was asked to be a speaker at the West Coast gathering of the Wild Goose Festival, with an invitation to basically come and talk about whatever I wanted to talk about.

Wild Goose Festival, which describes itself as "a community gathered at the intersection of justice, spirituality, music and art," is an amazing group that gathers each year to talk about faith, listen to music, and seek a better way forward. At the same time, my experience with many events that had drawn the same people, as well as my conversations with friends who were deeply involved in this movement of spirituality, justice, and arts, told me that race was still something that needed to be examined more thoroughly.

So, in the context of an event whose participants were predominately White, I chose to talk about race. But I wanted to talk about race differently — neither with a tone of "look how bad you White folks have been to us brown folks! Feel guilty, feel bad, and stop being racist" nor with an approach so analytical and academic that real-world application would be difficult. Plus, while some can powerfully talk about race girded by those postures, I really can't.

As happens so often, I was lying in bed when I

came up with an idea. I could list off things people have said to me that I felt were racially motivated at best and racist at worst, and then take some time to unpack each one. Once I decided on that method, sadly, the memories of what people had said to me just came pouring out, and I ended up with about ten original quotes.

The talk was well received, and about a month later, I was talking with a literary agent, trying to wrap my head around the complexities of the publishing world and licking my wounds from having another project turned down, and I suddenly thought about writing a book using this structure and publishing it myself.

I had published one book already with a startup e-publisher, Shook Foil books: *The Definitive-ish Guide for Using Social Media in the Church*, so I had a little experience with the process. With this knowledge about the speed, fiscal structures, and ease with which you can get a book into print and electronic forms, I figured that this was a great chance for me to dive into the self-publishing world.

The questions piled in my mind as I began to explore the possibilities. "Is this really just a way to avoid rejection from 'real' publishers?" "Do you really want to be one of those blowhards who thinks they are too good for the traditional publishing route, only to add one more crappy book to the pile of self-aggrandizement?" and most importantly, "Are you disciplined enough to do it?"

As I answered these questions for myself, I faced the fact that the last question was the most difficult one. I knew that even traditional publishers added crap to the bookshelves, and I was confident that if I networked enough, I could get *some* publishing house to take a chance on me. But that last issue I feared would get me. How was I going to self-publish a book when I was still expected to earn some money by speaking, teaching, and preaching, plus keep up with my blogging and be a good dad and husband? I thought that there was no way in H-E-double-hockey-sticks that I could also fit in a self-publishing project. No. Way.

And that's when Kickstarter (www.kickstarter.com) came onto my radar. Kickstarter is an online service that helps to build, support, give visibility to, and generate funding for creative projects. Helping the artist offer rewards for different levels of support and leverage personal relationships, the website helps "kickstart" projects like mine into action without the huge amount of personal resources that this would normally require of the artist.

I knew myself enough to know that, if I built the project in a way that would relieve some of the financial pressures that I was feeling *and* created a community of accountability, I just might be able to do it. So after doing a little more research, creating a timeline, and inviting a few folks into the process, I launched my first Kickstarter project, complete with a video introduction recorded by my eleven-year-old daughter, Abby.[16]

One of the most meaningful aspects of this book project was that, as a Kickstarter project, it represented a convergence of three deep passions in my life: my commitment to healthy social media usage, my dedication to practicing open-source discernment, and my belief that human beings are capable of having helpful and healthy conversations about race.

So, for the next few weeks, I cashed in my social credits, bombarded people with tweets, status updates,

---

[16] The original Kickstarter project page can be found at http://www.kck.st/RZT6Yx.

and emails, and basically poured my heart and soul into getting the project funded. Over time, many people helped spread the word, the support and pledges rolled in, and, at the end of the pledge window, the project ending up drawing 250 backers and was actually overfunded by nearly 25 percent.

When I received so much support, I was deeply grateful and humbled. At the same time, I could also feel a fogbank of anxiety beginning to blanket my spirit, because now, with 250 people waiting and watching — now I actually had to write the dang book.

So I began writing. I took a few weekend staycations to write, I wrote in coffee shops, on airplanes, sitting on my couch... pretty much wherever I could pop open my computer and put down a few words. At times, the words flowed out like water from a broken fire hydrant on a hot summer's day; at other times, I wondered if the word drought would ever end. I ended writing about 90 percent of it in the first month and was confident that I would make my self-imposed deadline.

Buzz. Incorrect. Thank you for playing.

I am not sure what it was, but for some reason, it just stopped. After that initial push, my writing mojo decreased, and the irresistible distractions increased. I ended up turning in the first draft more than a month late to Laura, my editor, and then was even more delayed in getting the manuscript back to her for the copy edit. In the meantime, Ryan had completed the cover art, Lauren was ready to start the publishing process, and I was beginning to get notes from people who were patient and kind, but who were asking, "Dude, where's my book?"

All the while, I kept telling myself and telling others, "Not too much longer, be patient, not too much longer." I am not sure why I thought the writing fairies would show up in the middle of the night and finish the book for me, but I kept waiting and they never showed up. I became a regular writer crying wolf.

The good news is that, if you are reading this now, I obviously overcame the procrastination and distractions and finished, fairies be damned.

In the end, I think that the blocks of time I spent away from the manuscript were good for me and, I hope, good for the final product. At least that's what I am going to tell myself and my great-grandchildren. Meanwhile, in comparison to a traditional publishing process, which can take years, this book's process took only about ten months from the idea's birth to the book's release. Not too bad in the grand scheme of things.

As I write this final part of the book, the publicity and marketing team (a.k.a me) is revving up its engines, poised start the social media and sales onslaught. I will seek reviews, find speaking gigs, and give interviews, all in the hopes that this book, one that I so deeply believe in, will make a difference in the world. I am excited about entering this stage of the project: going to events, engaging readers, and hoping to see some of the ideas I offer change the ways in which we talk to one another about race.

A friend who has been walking with me through this process asked me a few weeks ago, during one of the more difficult periods in the process, "Will you do this again?" At that moment, I could not imagine saying yes, as I wasn't sure that I would ever be finished with *this* project. That said, as I find myself finally on the other side of the self-publishing mountain, if the way be clear, the family willing, and the juices flowing, I probably will walk this road again in the future.

Until next time.

Kickstarted

I am profoundly grateful for everyone who has supported this project via Kickstarter and beyond.

I am particularly thankful for those who chose the reward that included answering the question, "Why should would talk about race?" Below are their responses as well as names and links to others who supported this project.

Please take a moment to visit some or all of these links as these are the folks who helped to make this book project possible, have wisdom to offer and want to continue to be a part of the conversation.

The Berman Family
Rick, Kathi, Kyle and Maria

Daughter adopted from Guatemala.

Now a multicultural family.

Live in a melting-pot city.

Opportunities for discord or harmony abound.

Talking leads to understanding,

releasing our diverse strengths

and empowering all who participate.

Irene Pak
twitter.com/ireney07

Because I'm tired of having explain that I am really from the United States. No, really.

Sarah L. Church

Among my fellow white people, the taboo around discussing race can prevent neighbors from getting to know each other across racial lines, and silence much-needed political debates. Talking about race is an important step toward greater connection between people, and greater political will to tackle deeply embedded structures of American and global inequality.

Christopher Brown

www.christopherbrown.wordpress.com

The Gospel calls Christians to crucify our racism and live in pursuit of reconciliation. Because many of us in the Church are ill-equipped to navigate the challenges of cross-cultural relationships, we need honest conversation about race to help the Church live the Gospel with integrity.

Derrick Weston

www.derricklweston.wordpress.com

To the extent that we are not discussing issues around race, we are closing ourselves off from hearing the stories of others. We need this conversation to help us develop compassion and empathy.

Mihee Kim-Kort

www.miheekimkort.com

These days, now that I'm a parent, I feel the need to raise awareness about race issues even more pressing. I want to be part of creating a culture that embraces constructive discourse about it. So, we have to talk about it.

Mary Ann Dimand

twitter.com/tressiemcphd

Silence endorses the current default—which remains one in which White folks are the norm from which others deviate. Without conversation that takes race and difference as glorious facts, we can neither come together, nor live honestly and well. Friends and partners can talk, and friends and partners do talk.

Sandra Mader

twitter.com/gago91107

Spend a couple of hours on a high school campus and you'll hear the racial slurs and epithets. Our children don't know how to relate to "those people." It's time to give them the tools to talk about race.

Stephen Salyards

www.blog.gajunkie.com

There are so many places in our daily lives that race plays a subtle and subconscious role. We need to be constantly in conversation with each other about this to have these places pointed out and hold each other accountable.

Josh Hale

twitter.com/expatminister

White is a race, too, and I'm less likely to own that unless I talk with others, alike and different, and keep it before me always—in ministry and personally.

Benjamin Howard

www.onpoptheology.com

Racial issues have played a large role in the history of our national conversation. From the Civil War to the civil rights movement, we have attempted to deal with racial issues through legislation and governmental power. However, this is not nearly enough. Legislation cannot fix these problems, but conversation can.

Jennifer Dawn Watts

twitter.com/jennwatts

Sixty-nine percent of problems in marriages are unsolvable. What keeps us out of gridlock is meaningful dialogue. Race seems to be one of those societal gridlocked issues that requires new ways to engage us in communication. Remaining unified isn't easy, but to understand each other better is really the key.

Lani Mah

Your racial identity is both a part of your heritage and your legacy. To truly know yourself, it is important to acknowledge, understand, and be proud of all that makes up who you are. Knowing your ancestry and understanding yourself will help you leave a richer legacy.

William Barnes
twitter.com/sayonaraML

Growing up in Massachusetts in the sixties meant never talking about race. We had seperate worlds, and I am unable to even remember having an African-American friend when I was growing up. I never even thought about race unless it was in sports and, in particular, Bill Russell, who was so amazingly erudite that I started paying attention to civil rights, and even then it was without context. As one of the invisible others (Canadian), anything that helps understanding is important.

Alycia Hwang

Because so many of us do not know the language to use.

Daniel So

twitter.com/headsparks

Our God-given diversity is something to celebrate, not ignore in the name of "color-blindness." The world in which my daughter lives is so diverse, and yet we continue to struggle with the same problems when it comes to race and ethnicity. We can, and must, shape a better future.

Landon Whitsitt

www.landonwhitsitt.com

For US Americans, an authentic understanding of race is the gateway to the Beloved Community.

Michael Landon

www.grieving-hearts-in-worship.com

From bullying and blatant discrimination to fear and ignorance of the unknown or unfamiliar, race plays a central role. We need to cultivate a healthy respect and genuine appreciation for one another, living the reality that we are all created in God's image; an important step in healing our world.

Karen Eng

Because it's the subtext of every human interaction, and greater awareness of how race informs how we ARE with one another enables us to be more genuinely WITH one another.

Martha Bettis Gee

Because racism underlies all our systems. If there is no honest dialogue about race, racism will remain an unacknowledged reality

Michael Adee

www.horizonsfoundation.org

Race matters. We cannot be silent about race, gender, sexual orientation, or any God-given difference. I grew up in segregated Louisiana, in a loving family and a faithful Presbyterian church. One's place with regard to race, gender, or sexual orientation was assumed. Superiority was clear: white, male, straight. Thank God the messages "You're a child of God, created, loved by God, just like everyone else" triumphed.

Lynn Hargrove

We look at the outside but God looks at the inside. May our eyes be opened to the beauty of the other.

Carol Dolezal-Ng

twitter.com/@caroliscreative

I have twins. One states, I am 1/2 Hawkeye (Iowan) and 1/2 Chinese! The other states I am 1/8 Irish, 1/8 Swiss, 1/4 Czechoslovakian, 1/2 Cantonese, and 100 percent American! Often I've been asked, "Where did they come from?" THEY are beloved children from God!

Mark Keonig

www.graybeardtrail.com

Race: a line we human beings draw to privilege some and disadvantage others. Talking about race is an essential step in the journey toward a world without lines, where privilege is no more, each person's dignity is affirmed, each person's value is honored, and justice and equality prevail.

Margaret Aymer

facebook.com/mayog

Race is the shibboleth that uncovers masked prejudices. For some, it invalidates cultural and geographic difference so that stereotypes may be assigned based on phenotype: all black people sing gospel, don't they? For others, race voids generations of living in the United States based on phenotype: no...where are you from?

And the rest of the Backers

To ensure the links from the 200+ backers stay current, rather than list each url in the print and electronic editions, all backers and their links can be found here:

http://goo.gl/meQOv

Salamat Po

Salamat po means "thank you" in Tagalog, the first language of my Filipino grandparents. The po represents an acknowledgment by the thanker of the honor and respect that should be given to the thankee.

I want to first thank my Jesus for... oh who am I kidding; I am not accepting a Grammy or celebrating a Super Bowl victory. Plus—just between me and you—I don't think Jesus really cares all that much if we publicly thank him for our achievements, so I'll start with my family. I am confident that the big JC will understand.

First, the humans who live in the same house as me deserve your sympathy and your applause.

To my wife of 20+ years, Robin, who had to deal with my inner and outer Mr. Angsty McAngsty during this entire process. When was stressing out about money, time, and the actual writing, she was there to helpfully ignore my whining and provide a quiet confidence that all would be okay.

To my daughters, Evelyn, Abby, and Annie, who for years have shared their dad with the larger community of people, conferences, and — during the writing of the books — coffee shops, I am grateful. *And girls, some day that parenting book will come, and you'll each get your chapter. ;-)*

To the nonhuman who served as a constant source of goofy pet antics, power-nap instigation and warm lap snuggling over the past year, Farah "Fawn" Fawncett, our dog, you have convinced me that small dogs aren't all that bad.

To the rest of my family[17]: Mom, Joel, Dad, Junie, Deanne, Lauren, Kevin, Ron, Beadle, Jessica, Wes, Henry, Barb, Lani, Robert, Tiffini, Trina, Kenneth, Cheri,

---

[17] My family tree is very complicated and requires a complex set of graphs and charts to explain, so you'll just have to trust me that these folks are, indeed, family.

Ham, Judy, Tammie, Ricky, the assorted nieces and nephews and [insert forgotten relatives here], thank you for picking up the slack while I have been gallivanting around town and calling it work.

To those in San Francisco who have stepped up and shown what it means to be community: thank you! From spontaneous conversations over coffee to soccer-game sideline bonding and to helping make sure that we did not forget to pick up a child — Stephanie, Rick, Kathi, Kelly, Gigi, Paul, Donna, Jon, Rose, Alberta, Leslie, and the rest — you are amazing and we are blessed to have you as an extension of our family and community.

Then there are those groups and individuals for whom I am also deeply grateful, most probably have no idea how much their friendship, presence, and support have meant to me during this time: Seventh Avenue Presbyterian Church, the Urban Pastors' Group, the Filipino American National Historical Society, Trinity Presbyterian Church, Mission Bay Community Church, the Presbyterian Peacemaking Program, Montreat Youth Conferences, David, Eliacin, Rick, Mark, Nancy, Nadia, Francis, Neal, Mienda, Byron, Margaret, Tara, Stephanie, Derrick, Abby, and so many more.

And finally the team who helped to make this book come to life: Laura, Lauren and Ryan.

Laura Garwood Meehan, Editor — Laura's deft handling of this writer's fragile ego was a sight to behold. I often found myself smirking as I read through her critiques, affirmations, and suggestions as she peppered them with wit, insight, and care. I am grateful for her voice in the process, and while I will miss our ongoing interactions, I will not miss her editing voice whispering in my ear: "dense and abstract, dense and abstract." Find out more about Laura and her work at www.laurameehan.com and www.indigoediting.com.

Lauren Reyes Gibbs, Publishing — Lauren, who doubles as my younger sister and a stunning writer in her own right, was, as expected, thorough and diligent throughout the process. Considering how much she had to put up with her older brother's creative understanding of deadlines, I am grateful for her competency, patience and care. Read her story on her blog: www.dearestdaughters.com.

Ryan Kemp-Pappan, Cover Design — Ryan did not hesitate when I asked if he would be willing to be part of this project, and I hope he is not sorry he said yes.

With scant artistic guidance or design direction from me, and no less than six title changes over the span of the project, Ryan maintained his flexibility and creativity throughout the entire process. Of course, my name might have been taken in vain a few times, but ah, well, from Ryan, I consider that a badge of honor. You can find Ryan's blog and artwork at www.beingRKP.com.

I end this thank you with a word of deep gratitude to God who I believe has been present and active, not only through those whom I have already mentioned, but also in the subtle, still and silent ways that I never had expected and only God could do.

Salamat po,

Stay in Touch

I would love to keep in touch with folks, so if you want stay connected or if you need to get in touch with me, below are the best ways to do so.

The Basics

- Send me things in paper form to:
  1728 Ocean Avenue #204, San Francisco, CA 94112

- I'm not the best responder, but feel free to email me:
  breyeschow@gmail.com

- The main hub of information about me:
  www.reyes-chow.com

- Sign up for my regular e-newsletter:
  mad.ly/signups/29509/join

- Feel free to tinker and update my Wikipedia page: en.wikipedia.org/wiki/Bruce_Reyes-Chow

- Follow me on Twitter: www.twitter.com/breyeschow

- Like my Facebook page: www.facebook.com/breyeschowpage

- See my daily pictures on Instagram: www.facebook.com/breyeschowpage

- Watch my videos on YouTube www.youtube.com/breyeschow

- Add me to a circle on Google+: plus.google.com/u/0/116068780296930090249

- Connect with me on LinkedIn www.linkedin.com/in/breyeschow

- Pin with me on Pinterest: www.pinterest.com/breyeschow

For my bio, current projects and contact information

www.reyes-chow.com

About Bruce

Bruce is a native Northern Californian and 3rd generation Chinese/Filipino who writes and speaks extensively on faith, politics, race and technology.

Bruce graduated from San Francisco State University with a degree in Philosophy, Sociology and Asian American studies, earned his masters degree from San Francisco Theological Seminary and was granted an honorary Doctor of Divinity degree from Austin College.

The author of *The Definitive-ish Guide for Using Social Media in the Church*, for the past 20 years he has worked with groups and individuals in areas of social justice, church planting, technology and diversity.

Bruce lives in San Francisco, CA with his wife, Robin, his three daughters, Evelyn, Abby and Annie and one very cute canine.

Pup E. Chow

Pup E. Chow

I really like animals. I
especially love dogs.